THINGS I NEVER SAID

Emails to my African American Son in College

Essays

by

Jay Thomas Willis

INFINITY PUBLISHING

ISBN 0-7414-5994-9

Printed in the United States of America

Published December 2010

INFINITY PUBLISHING
1094 New DeHaven Street, Suite 100
West Conshohocken, PA 19428-2713
Toll-free (877) BUY BOOK
Local Phone (610) 941-9999
Fax (610) 941-9959
Info@buybooksontheweb.com
www.buybooksontheweb.com

DEDICATION

To all Black fathers who wish to establish better relationships with their sons.

PREFACE

The day my son went away to college I decided to send him an email once a week. I kept a log of these emails and eventually put them into this book, hoping that what I had to say would be of benefit to him as well as some other African American children and their fathers. I felt this would provide some helpful information for him, and provide a relief for me as well. Writing these emails was a form of therapy.

I wrote one email a week for the first two semesters he was in college to get him off to a good start. It's never too late, and I was determined to have an influence on my son's life. So I took this opportunity to attempt a redevelopment of our father and son relationship.

My ancestors passed on communication difficulties because of slavery. This led to communication problems between my father and I, which consequently led to communication problems between my son and I. In addition, I had some unique communication difficulties of my own. Communication is a higher-order need. One usually doesn't think about communication until lower-level needs are taken care of. My ancestors spent most of their time trying to attain basic things like food, clothing, and shelter. The rest of their time was spent on safety issues. Very little time was given to a higher-order need like communication.

I sent these emails to my son, but I didn't know if he would take the time to read all of them—I could only hope. But I continued to send them to him. My son can be rather obstreperous and stubborn if something is not his idea. I gave thought to the idea that he might have seen these emails as an intrusion on his life, and decided not to waste his time reading them. Because of our lack of communication, I sometimes think he feels I have absolutely nothing of value to say. It all comes from our lack of communication in the past. But he assured me that he had read all of them.

I wanted to say to him all that I had been unable to say to him while growing up, and some other things I thought might be of value to him.

All of these emails are about things that I assume my son was not aware. If I thought he was aware of them I wouldn't have mentioned them.

I wanted to have my son respond to each email, but then I realized how much I'd be imposing on his time. I'd then be defeating my purpose, for he needed to concentrate on his studies. I decided to simply let the emails consist of expressing my point of view. My son hasn't discovered the writing talent that lies deep within his soul.

Every effort has been made to prevent repetition, but due to the nature of the book, it is almost impossible to avoid repetition of some of the more familiar themes. In some places I considered repetition good for emphasis, in order to get across a consistent and centralized point of view. Again, if I repeat myself it's because of the necessity to tell a complete story in each email, and certain themes about my life keep reappearing. When first I began to improve my conscious level, it took a lot of repetition before certain things would sink in. I figured it to be the same with my son. I hope it's not too awkward for the reader.

This book is necessary reading for African American college students, teenagers, and their parents. Especially all African American fathers should read this book.

ACKNOWLEDGMENT

Thanks to my son Martin for being willing to receive these emails. This gave the author motivation to continue writing. Martin generally regards such sentimental efforts as foolish.

CONTENTS

ABOUT THE AUTHOR

JAY THOMAS WILLIS is a graduate of the University of Houston, Houston, Texas where he earned a Master's degree in social work; he is also a graduate of the Master's degree counseling program at Texas Southern University, Houston, Texas. He attended undergraduate school at Stephen F. Austin State University, Nacogdoches, Texas where he earned a B.S. degree in sociology and social and rehabilitative services.

He worked as a Clinical Social Worker for seventeen years, providing direct clinical services as well as supervision. He has been a consultant to a nursing home and a boys group home; taught college courses in sociology, family, and social work in community college and university settings; and has worked as a family therapist for several agencies in the Chicago area. In addition, he was a consultant to a number of home-health care agencies in the south suburbs and Chicago. Mr. Willis is a past CHAMPUS peer reviewer for the American Psychological Association and the American Psychiatric Association. He also spent a number of years in private practice as a Licensed Clinical Social Worker in the State of Illinois.

Mr. Willis has traveled and lectured extensively on the condition of the African American community. He has written twenty-one books, and written many Journal articles on the subject of the African American community. He has written several magazine articles. He has also written Op-Ed Commentaries for the *Chicago Defender*, *Final Call*, *East Side Daily News* of Cleveland, and *Dallas Examiner*. He currently lives in Richton Park, Illinois with his wife and son.

ALSO BY JAY THOMAS WILLIS

Nonfiction
A Penny for Your Thoughts: Insights, Perceptions, and Reflections on the African American Condition

Implications for Effective Psychotherapy with African Americans

Freeing the African-American's Mind

God or Barbarian: The Myth of a Messiah Who Will Return to Liberate Us

Finding Your Own African-Centered Rhythm

When the Village Idiot Get Started

Nowhere to Run or Hide

Why Blacks Behave as They Do: The Conditioning Process from Generation to Generation

God, or Balance in the Universe

Over the Celestial Wireless

Paranoid but not Stupid

Nothing but a Man

ALSO BY JAY THOMAS WILLIS

Fiction
You Can't Get There from Here

Where the Pig Trail Meets the Dirt Road

The Devil in Angelica

As Soon as the Weather Breaks

The Cotton is High

Hard Luck

Educated Misunderstanding

Poetry
Reflections on My Life: You're Gonna Carry That Weight a Long Time

August 26, 2009

1

The Hunted

If you don't mind, I need your permission to send you no more than one email every week. If you read my emails you are guaranteed to become a stronger African American man; one that will stay in the tradition of maintaining a strong family. It might take a while for you to understand what I'm trying to say; even though you are much more exposed than I was at your age. If they don't help you, bare with me, it will help me in so many ways to get the information off my chest. I want to send you some words of motivation and encouragement.

I hope what I have to say in these emails will help you to become the man I was never able to be. I feel you need my perspective. Whether you believe it or not at this point, as you progress in school you will find what I say more acceptable.

I hope you read my emails over the next year as you matriculate in college. If you don't I will understand. I know there is a tendency for you to say, I already know that, or this is ridiculous. But try and read what I have to say. I think you will find what I say interesting. You might be tempted to say, "I haven't listened to this guy all these years, why should I listen to him now?"

I hope you don't mind my using this opportunity to say some of the things I couldn't say to you in person as you grew up. To tell the truth I didn't think you were ready for this kind of information, and I was afraid you wouldn't receive it well. I believe I can say it better when it is impersonal.

It was hard for me to express my feelings to you because my father had difficulty expressing himself to me. It is said that such things get passed on from one generation to another. They say Black fathers don't talk to their sons like they should. Much of it has to do with the disconnection that occurred in slavery between the Black male and his family. Because of my history, I'm sure I was not there for you, I realize that; either socially or emotionally. That also has to do with my father not being there for me. That is in part why the Black family finds itself today in such a difficult position. Black men have traditionally not been available emotionally, socially, or financially for their sons or daughters.

You are a young eager Black man, and probably think you are playing on a level playing field, but you will soon find that the cards are stacked against you. That's why in the past only a few Black men have been successful at negotiating the system. The system has been set up that way. You have to be talented, play your cards right, and get some tremendous opportunities in order to be a successful Black man. I don't want to discourage you but to motivate you. By getting a good education you will possibly be one of those successes, but you have to keep all aspects of your life in balance. It seems that Obama has been able to do this, although you can be a success without being President.

I know you haven't been the victim of a great deal of racism, and when you have you probably weren't aware of it. Young people are conditioned to ignore racism. But now that you are out in the world, chances are you will be exposed to prejudice and racism, in ways that will be impossible to ignore. When you face racism and prejudice you must keep your head held high, your chest out, and stare it directly in the face. Don't ever let it get the best of you. You must always stand up and be a man, don't run from it.

If you haven't encountered racism already, after being in college only a few days, it's time that you learned about it.

Neely Fuller, Jr. an activist for Blacks said, "If you don't understand racism—what it is—and what it does, everything else you know, or think you know, will only confuse you."

Throughout history, other groups have been determined to prevent the rise of a Black Messiah. Check history out for yourself. That's why they killed Dr. Martin Luther King, Jr. and Malcolm X. That is also in part why they refuse to do anything about the educational, political, social, and economic systems; and in part why they have treated Blacks so poorly throughout history.

I know Obama is President, and a lot of other groups bend over backward to be cordial and respectful, but we indeed have a long way to go in terms of improving race relations. Even other groups with the best intentions are conditioned to look upon you with some disdain.

Some think because of Obama, prejudice and racism will be reduced. That is because other groups now get an up close and personal view of an intelligent, educated, and articulate African American man. They believe this is enough to change the nature of prejudice in this country. I happen to disagree with this assessment; it is contrary to American history. America has gone through many cycles, where it improves for a while, and then gets worse. There has been no straight-linear progress throughout the history of this country for Blacks.

Now that we have Obama as President, you will probably see a backlash. Instead of things getting better for Blacks, you will find they will get worse. This has to do with the fact that other groups will try to crack down on the possibility of the rise of any more Obamas. They at least would like to limit the number of Black men who could potentially become successful. Why? Because that is the way things have always been; but it is no reason for them to continue that way.

There is a poem that you should be familiar with. It talks about how a pig is hunted by men and hounds and penned. It says in short that if we are to be hunted, we must not be like that stuck-penned pig, but we must fight back in a dignified manner, and not just be hunted and killed with no dignity. We must go down gloriously, if we indeed are to be hunted. The poem is by Claude McKay, and called "If We Must Die."

> If we must die, let it not be like hogs
> Hunted and penned in an inglorious spot,
> While round us bark the mad and hungry dogs,
> Making their mock at our accursed lot.
> If we must die, O let us nobly die,
> So that our precious blood may not be shed
> In vain; then even the monsters we defy
> Shall be constrained to honor us though dead!
> O kinsmen! We must meet the common foe!
> Though far outnumbered let us show us brave,
> And for their thousand blows deal one death-blow!
> What though before us lies the open grave?
> Like men we'll face the murderous, cowardly pack,
> Pressed to the wall, dying, but fighting back!

Being the bright-intelligent person you are, for which I would like to take some responsibility, you might think my emails are stupid. But if you just read them now, I assure you that in a few years you will find them anything but stupid. For some reason, in the past, when I have tried to talk to you, you looked at me as if I was a stranger with another stupid idea.

I will quit now because I don't want you to use time reading my emails when you could be studying. I am concerned about the length of my emails, because the last thing I want to do is bore you. My time is almost up, it is time for you to carry on, and the whole world can be yours if you play your cards right.

Be patient with me, I promise to keep the emails short, and it will be my way of keeping in touch. I hope this is not too much to ask.

The purpose of my emails is to get you to laugh every now and then, and to give you something positive to focus on while dealing with all the negativity. I'm interested in your survival as a student and as a person.

Be steadfast!!!!!!!!!!!

September 2, 2009

2

College Do's and Don'ts

These are some do's and don'ts that you should consider. I want to help make your college experience a success. I know you're aware of many of these things; I just want to remind you. My emails will be geared toward making your college experience a success. These are just a few things off the top that, if I had adhered to, would've made my college experience better. Keep in mind that there's a right way to do things. Whether you do them right or wrong makes all the difference in the world.

(1). Set your alarm clock so you get up on time for classes.

(2). There's a solution to every problem, don't let any problem overly frustrate you. Remember there's always an alternative.

(3). If you have a problem getting up early for classes, in the future schedule your classes for later in the day.

(3). Get involved in other activities besides classes: such as clubs, organizations, and fraternities. For this world one needs to be well rounded. Social activities are needed; don't stay in your room all the time isolated.

(4). Don't be late or tardy for any class unless absolutely necessary; if you have to be late on one occasion, just don't make a habit of it. Being late or tardy is one of the worse offenses you could commit—professors get very upset.

(5). Another bad offense in college you shouldn't commit is to go to class and nod off in class. Professors get the idea that you're not a serious student.

(6). Never argue with a professor in class. If you must argue with him or her, go to his or her office in private and discuss it. This is another of the bad offenses.

(7). You can use your own judgment, but some instructors give you a grade partially based upon your participation in class. Some classes are strictly a lecture format and no participation is required. His syllabus should specify these details. Be sure and understand the syllabus for each class.

(8). Do what the instructor ask you to do, and get your assignments in on time.

(9). In the future, if you get a chance, find out about a professor before you take his class. Instructors are just like other people, they're not all the same. Some will make your life miserable, even in the so-called same class. Some are ridiculous in their requirements.

(10). Don't worry about working the first or second semester. Use your time for getting adjusted and maintaining your grades.

(11). Be aware of predators, there're all kind of predators out there. Don't get involved in an undesirable relationship.

(12). Take the best notes you can. Read over these notes before the next class—if possible. Also, rewrite your notes so they're plain and clear. Read the chapter assigned before class if you can, and read any other assignments before class. Study as you go along during the semester, so you won't have to cram at the last minute. If you have a lab, be sure you go over the material in the lab book prior to the next lab.

(13). You only have a certain amount of time. Learn to manage your time well.

(14). Students function at all different levels. Be sure you recognize your individual needs for study.

(15). Don't raise your voice at people unless they're attempting to violate you in some way. Keep an even respectful tone.

(16). Unless you know someone very well, and I'd be careful even then, don't loan your property to anyone. People have a general tendency to be lax about returning things.

(17). Don't stay out late. Come in so you won't be sleepy, late, or tardy for your next day classes.

(18). Make the library your friend. Know where resources are in the library, and generally where the various categories of books are located. Read the local and national newspaper, and a national newsweekly such as Time or Newsweek magazine. At least watch the news on TV. Keep up with what's going on locally and in the larger world. This will help to make your college experience a better one. This is why you don't need to focus on working. Use your time to enrich yourself.

(19). Don't waste too much time sleeping. Remember, nothing comes to a sleeper but a dream; always get up and go to your classes. Remember what Nas says "Sleep is the cousin of death." No need to lie there sleeping when you know you need to get up, get breakfast, go to class and study. *The early bird gets the worm.* Benjamin Franklin said once in the eighteen hundreds: *Early to bed, early to rise; makes one healthy, wealthy, and wise.*

(20). Always utilize good home training, be courteous and respectful to others. But don't let anyone push you around. This is necessary in a concentrated college living environment.

(21). Get started and finish any term papers long before the deadline. Be sure you have time to proofread your papers several times. This will keep you from making many typographical and other errors. Never wait until the last minute and have to rush your papers.

(22. Always be sure when you leave the campus that you have a ride back to the campus, and be careful who you ride with. Don't just jump in the car with anyone.

(23). Don't sell any course short by not giving it proper time, study, and attention.

(24). Don't wait until the middle of the semester to realize you need to do more studying, jump on the books at the beginning and ride them for the entire semester. You know you sometimes have a tendency to start off slow and try to play catch up later on—don't do that.

(25). Sometimes it's hard, but try to get to know your instructors on a personal level. If you do, when you're on the borderline between a "B" and a "C" you'll be more likely to get the "B."

(26). Try to be present for 100% of your classes. Don't depend on anyone to take notes for you. And always take the best notes you can.

(27). Stay away from drugs and alcohol, and always be positive.

(28). Black males have a high college drop-out rate, and are expected to fail in some cases. They claim Black males don't have what it takes to matriculate in college. In your case, I want you to prove them wrong.

(29). Everyone should be interested in making friends, but if someone clearly indicates they don't want to be your friend, put some distance between yourself and the person.

(30). Hang out with positive people; stay clear of negative people.

(31). You can accomplish anything you want, but you must be organized to do so. Whatever you do, keep yourself and your studies organized.

(32). When you're reading on a daily basis, if you run across a word you don't know the meaning, look it up in the dictionary. This will serve to increase your vocabulary in the long run. A good vocabulary is a strong point in mainstream society.

(33). Don't let what another student say diminish your self-esteem or self-worth, no matter who it is. Students in your classes will come from many different places, and have all kinds of ideas. Many of their ideas won't be favorable.

When I was a student, both professors and students said many negative things about Blacks. Much of it was hurtful to me, and I wasn't prepared for their comments. Always consider the source: Where're they from? What're their objectives? What ideas are they trying to push? What's their modus operandi?

I can tell you about a lot of things, but can only give you an abstract notion of how to relate to people. My skills in that area are poor, because I don't have that much actual experience.

I'll never be happy until you accomplish your lifetime objectives. I've probably already gotten what I'm going to get out of life.

If you follow these basic rules you'll find yourself having a much better college experience. Remember your home training, and always try to do what's right.

Be kind to yourself!!!!!!!!!!

September 9, 2009

3

Why the Urgency to Party and Have a Good Time?

I know many things I'm going to tell you, you'll say, "I already know that." Sometimes I know you say this simply to get me off your back. I believe this to be true, because you say you already know, and continue to act as if you didn't have the faintest idea about what I said. Well, I'm just reminding you of things you already know, if indeed you are already aware of them.

Some teenagers go to college and feel too much of a need to party and have a good time. They feel they're in college to have a good time, and forget their real purpose for being in college. I can see the need to have a good social life, and students should have an enjoyable time, but you don't need to party like the world is coming to an end. If you live your life right you'll have plenty of time to party.

I wish I had spent more of my time reading and studying, both in elementary, junior high, high school, and college. I can understand why teenagers feel pressure to party. When I was in school I ran the streets like it was nobody's business. I just had to be where the action was, and chasing the girls. My hormones were acting up, and I felt compelled to stay on the prowl. I did that even though I had many deficits.

I had to work on the farm a lot in elementary, junior high, and high school; but I could have spent some quiet evenings, holidays, and late nights reading up on what I needed to know. In this way, even though my teachers were providing me with an inadequate education, I could have maintained my competitive edge.

My situation was different from yours. My education from elementary, junior high, and high school was vastly inadequate. It was up to me, and teachers didn't try to be sure I was learning anything. You probably got a fairly good education at Sieden Prairie and Rich South. My education was full of deficits. As you probably know, the more deficits you carry over from secondary school, the harder it'll be in college. You should be aware of where you are educationally, and what your educational needs are. I was so isolated and ignorant that I wasn't even aware of how much I didn't know. In high school I thought the less pressure on the part of teachers, the better off I was. My parents also didn't seem to care if I learned anything or not. They didn't even have the skills to monitor my progress in school. My mother and father never once came to the school to see how I was doing.

The important thing is to realize what your deficits are, so you can spend some extra time, if you have any, trying to catch up on those deficits. My deficits were so great when I got to college that I had to spend what time I had, when I wasn't in the streets, reading what I was assigned. I had no time for reading newspapers, magazines (Time, Newsweek), or looking at news on TV. You'll find that it's important to keep up with these things. This will even help you out with some of your classes. Some professors will throw in a few questions from their lectures as they relate to current events—on his test. If you don't keep up with current events you'll find it hard to relate to the professor's questions. Sometimes the lecture will address current events. To understand what is being said, you need to understand these events.

It's also good to keep up with current events, because if you don't, when you meet people you'll seem like a "dud" if you don't know what's going on locally and in the national news. You'll even find that other students on campus will frequently use current events as a desired and preferred topic of discussion. If you don't keep up with these events you'll be considered undesirable as a friend, and find it difficult to engage in their conversations.

So avoid this urgency to excessively party and have a good time. Socialize for sure, but keep you mind on your studies. You know what you're there for, and must take advantage of this opportunity. You're not missing a great deal in the world or in Chicago for that matter, by being in college. Don't worry about what your friends are doing, if they're smart, they'll be doing the same thing you should be doing: trying to make a better future for yourself.

You can't wait until the last minute of the semester to get organized and get focused. If you wait you might wait too late. Make it a practice to get to work early in the semester, and keep up with your studies. Never give up!

Be courageous and inspired!

September 16, 2009

4

College Requires More Study Than High School

Don't feel college is going to be similar to high school. College is going to require much more independent study. You are going to have to do some serious study, if you are to do well. I'm sure you've found that out already.

It doesn't matter how intelligent you are, you still have to study hard. Marcus was intelligent enough, but didn't make it at Urbana. The reason was because, I think he spent too much time sleeping, not going to class, and not studying. I don't know that for a fact, but believe it to be so. He wasn't use to studying hard—I don't think. No matter what you did in high school, college requires intense study.

I cautioned Marcus to take some general courses his first and second semester until he could get adjusted, not jump in on what the Computer Engineering program specified, but he wouldn't listen to me.

When I was talking to Marcus, Frances told me that Marcus had a different background than I had, and that he should be able to make it. I knew it was going to be difficult for him. It's difficult enough without the professors trying to make it hard. At a school like Urbana they sometimes deliberately make it difficult—especially in something like Computer Engineering.

In your case they had the program already set up for you, and it didn't seem that unreasonable. That's why I didn't say anything to you about what you were taking. I did keep asking you what you were taking. And I suggested that you take some speech if at all possible.

Remember that most of the kids in college are intelligent, not exactly like high school, and everybody is going to be hustling for grades. Competition for grades in college is tough. You must stay focused on paying attention in class, studying, and doing your assignments. In spite of your decent background it will require hard work. You must understand that some kids are better prepared than you are, but you can beat them by working hard. Your willingness to work hard will determine how well you do

When I was in elementary, junior high, and high school, we didn't get enough homework; we got a little but not nearly enough. I remember doing only one paper and reading only one book for those 12 years. We didn't even go on field trips. We didn't do much of anything. I rarely used the library. I didn't have enough sense to read on my own. I thought I was getting over on the teachers. It turns out that I was the fool. I thought my teachers were suckers, but I was the biggest sucker.

I know you worked hard in high school and throughout your school years. And I don't want you to feel you can quit now, because you are virtually on your own. They say a man's true character is determined by what he does when no one else is watching. I hope you don't need Frances and I to watch over you to get you to do your assignments and study.

When I went to college I didn't know how poorly I was prepared for college. You are probably much better prepared than I was, but you will still have to work hard. All I had was ambition, and I was going to do whatever it took to get me through. Luckily, I made it. But I didn't make it without studying hard. I won't try and tell you how to study, but there is a secret to knowing how to study. Everybody has an approach that works best for them. You should soon find out what works best for you. At least that's what you should be trying to do.

For example, I always told you to read any novel twice: once using broad strokes, and again for details. Do your math assignments every night, and practice working problems before the test. Always study your notes, and read all assigned material. If you have a paper to do, get it done in plenty of time in order to proofread it, form a partnership—get a friend to proofread it. You can always email it to me, and I will proofread it for you.

Frances had a better academic background than I had, yet she didn't do as well as she would like to have the first few years. It took her a while to catch on. Again, you have to know how and when to study. I think she was trying to keep up with the social crowd. There's no way around studying in college if you hope to do well in your grades.

Some students drop out of college because they are not willing to study like they should. Some would rather go off and join the Army than spend their time studying in college. I saw it happen many times. There are those who would rather take any kind of a job rather than stay in college and study. Whatever you do don't quit. Don't make a bad habit of quitting. It's always easier to give up and not do anything worthwhile, but is it worth it.

In regard to Urbana: think about this. You can run but you can't hide. Don't think that Urbana is going to be any better as far as people go. The people at Springfield are a cross section of the nation. You are going to find the same kind of people at Urbana. You may as well get your feet wet at Springfield. Think about getting enough credits to be a junior, and then transferring.

What you do now will help to determine your future. So don't slack off. Get to work and treat every day as if it is the first day of the rest of your life, and is important. One man said, "Shoot for the moon, and if you clear the fence, you'll be doing fine. In other words, strive for an "A" and it you make a "B," you'll be in good shape.

You can hang out with your friends, but know when it's time to study.

Be considerate!!!!!!!!!!!!!!!

September 23, 2009

5

My Assignment

Ministers say every living soul was put on this earth with a purpose in mind. Some can do a number of things well, while others can master at least one thing. Some are better at some things than others. Some people can sing, others can dance, while others can play an instrument, others are good at sports; and there are many other things people are good at. While you were growing up I didn't notice what you were good at. But I did notice that you are generally a highly intelligent individual, who could potentially master any number of academic areas. I did notice that you could potentially be good with computers. Computers are basic to every field these days. It's up to you what area you choose to develop. Whatever you choose, work at it, and master it. The sky is the limit for you.

You need to find out what your assignment is. What are you good at, and what are you most comfortable doing? Find out and spend your time developing in this area. Don't waste your time at something completely alien to your nature, and don't wait until you are old and grey before trying to develop in your assignment.

No one can tell you what this assignment is, it's up to you to discover and develop this talent. School is supposed to help you to find this assignment by exposing you to many different areas. Others can suggest areas to you based on your performance in certain areas, but only you know what you enjoy, and are most comfortable at. Money is another consideration. Don't take up something that you know will not support your lifestyle.

Ministers and others say you won't be happy until you're doing what God placed you here to do. Not many people carry out their assignments. That's the way the system is set up. In many cases the system doesn't help people to find out their assignments—especially those provided with an inadequate education. Many people end up doing what someone else wanted them to do, or what was more convenient for them to get into. Most people take the shortest distance between a straight line. But don't be duped by what comes easiest. Where there is no struggle there is no progress.

I didn't know what to major in. I wanted to major in pre-pharmacy, but the program was more difficult than I thought. The pre-pharmacy curriculum was rather rigorous. My background hadn't prepared me in chemistry. So I took something in which I could achieve a passing grade. There were many subjects I could have done well in besides social work.

I got into social work by trying to avoid everything people told me was difficult. By a process of elimination I ended up with social work. Social work should have been the last subject I majored in. Social work would have been more suitable for a minor rather than a major.

I think writing is my assignment on this earth, after I spent over half my life in social work. I got side tracked because I didn't have enough exposure to writing. I feel that with some additional training at a younger age I could have been a decent writer. But I was fifty-years old before even considering writing. This is late but not too late. I don't want you to wait that long before you figure out what you're good at. The earlier you start in your assignment the more you have a chance to develop it.

Try to find out what you're good at, cultivate it, and master it. The world is not like "I Dream of Jeanie," you can't wink and get what you want; you've got to work at it.

You will be much happier with your life. Work consumes a large portion of a person's life. Most people are unhappy with their lives, the reason is because they are doing something they don't enjoy, something totally alien to their assignment.

There are many occupations in this world. Most people go a lifetime without learning about most of them. They simply take what is available locally. But there is no reason why you can't find out your assignment and work at developing it.

College is for the purpose of giving you a foundation so you can have the general skills to do what you want to do. Don't let a degree in a particular field limit you in what you want to do. No matter what you major in you can use it to help you carry out your assignment. But if you're sure that your chosen field is what you want to pursue then by all means do so with all your heart and soul.

Remember that drugs and alcohol will permit people to take advantage of you, and will put you in an embarrassing position. I have seen people robbed and sexually taken advantage of while using drugs and alcohol. You want to always maintain control of your faculties. Drugs and alcohol will prevent you from mastering your assignment.

Be intuitive!!!!!!!!!!

September 30, 2009

6

Communication

If I repeat myself from time to time it's because some things are worth repeating.

Some say the reason why apes haven't progressed any further is they don't have the ability to verbally communicate. Once an ape learns that he can take a stick and retrieve a banana, he can't pass on this knowledge in the form of written or oral knowledge to the next generation. Each generation of apes must go through a similar process of trial and error in order to figure out how to get the task done. They can't store or keep records so that each new generation can learn from the efforts of past generations. In this case they wouldn't have to waste a lot of time relearning what should already be part of the group's skills.

If Black parents don't communicate to their children, it puts them in a similar situation as apes. If nothing is being passed on, each new generation has to go through a type of trial and error learning process on any given problem. Each generation has to go for themselves. We're slowly going the way of the apes. The more we don't communicate, the less we will be able to communicate. This skewed communication process accounts for some of our lack of progress.

The problem with communication in the Black family began over 10,000 years ago, when other groups first set foot on the African continent. I don't have space or time to tell the whole story; you must be motivated to read some of this history for yourself. But don't let me sidetrack you; concentrate on your assigned readings.

When other groups appeared on the shores of Africa they made us feel as though our culture was inferior and theirs was superior. We allowed them to take some control of the functioning of our institutions. Before we knew what was happening they had taken complete control, and began to dismantle our social, political, economic, marital, and educational institutions. We went into a state where we lost our norms and became confused. At this point our communication with each other began to break down. We were then vulnerable when the slave trade came along.

During the Middle Passage we were divided by language, culture, and tribe on the trek to the ships, and again on the ships. Once we were on the shores of America we were divided again by culture, language, and tribe. It made communication almost impossible. Then in slavery we were sent from plantation to plantation for sale purposes, without regard for family ties. Black males were used for breeding purposes, and were not allowed to take responsibility for their offspring. Men couldn't be responsible husbands and fathers.

We were not allowed to assemble in numbers greater than two, either on the plantation or in the cities. We were not allowed to travel from plantation to plantation without express written permission. This limited our ability to communicate with one another, and our ability to form any kind of a rebellion. These rules were strictly enforced.

All this disruption put the finishing touches on our communication. In this process we lost our ability to meaningfully communicate with one another, something we have been trying to regain ever since. At this time we've lost all semblance of family communication. In some cases still today, not only with parent and child, but several Black people can be talking and understanding the same message differently. They won't have the slightest idea about what the other is talking about, even though they understand some of the words.

The inability to communicate from parent to child has been passed on from generation to generation. It proves even more difficult for fathers to communicate with their sons, because of the psychology involved. Some older generations felt so alienated and frustrated that they gave up trying to communicate with their children.

My father was one of those who had this heritage passed on to him. He therefore never tried to establish any meaningful communication with me. They say if your father never tried or failed to establish communication with you, it will be hard for you to establish communication with your son(s). I think that's why I failed to establish wholesome communication with you.

There is an old saying, *the buck stops here*. Meaning, at this point the disturbed communication must end. I would like to make some inroads into the destructive father to son communication patterns in our family. It must begin with your generation.

In addition to having a father who didn't communicate with me, no one else in my family made an effort to communicate with me. Part of my problem was that I stuttered so badly that no one wanted to be bothered with me. Even people outside the family would ask my parents, sisters, or brothers questions about me, rather than talk to me directly. I ended up having people talk at me, rather than engaging in a communication process with me. You'll notice when I'm around people I usually listen rather than engage in conversation. That's an old time-worn habit. Consequently, I have never felt comfortable communicating with anyone. You can see how my communication would be a bit skewed. This is another reason why I never communicated with you as much and as effectively as I should have. I learned to avoid spoken communication altogether for a long time.

Here we go with the old story! On top of that, I spent most of my childhood in isolation. We lived at the end of a three-mile trail that only a wagon or horse could negotiate. We didn't get a dirt road constructed until I was seven-years old. There were very few people to communicate with back in those woods. I also never had an opportunity to get involved in speech therapy once I started school. There was no such thing as speech therapy at our school. My first speech course was in college, and by then it was almost too late to help improve my speech.

Of course, some families are better at this communication than others, as with most situations. It is hard even for those who have had conditions favorable for communication. Different families start at different places. But Black parents, Black fathers especially, must begin to communicate with their sons. As I said, some situations are worse than others. The reason for much violence, incarceration, and drugs has to do with absent fathers and lack of father to son communication. Young men need to see Black fathers leading in the family, and constantly trying to improve communication with them.

I hope that we can get our communication on the right track. And you will be able to more effectively communicate with your son(s).

Be studious!!!!!!

October 7, 2009

7

Choosing Your Friends

Everybody need friends, you can't exist in this world alone. If you try to exist alone you'll have a lonely existence. You need to be involved in a mutual support network. Although, everybody you meet won't turn out to be your friend.

At some point, especially in today's world, you'll be confronted with picking and choosing who your friends should be. We live in a multi-ethnic, multi-cultural, and multi-racial society. For one to choose their friends strictly because they're Black might be a mistake. On the other hand, to reject them because they're not Black might be another mistake. In today's world one must pick and choose their friends based on their personalities rather than on race, religion, or ethnic origin.

Some Blacks have been conditioned to self-hate in many situations. It'll be rather difficult to get along with anyone who hates himself, and one with such self-hate will have a difficult time enjoying a relationship with someone with the same qualities as they have.

They turn all their frustrations and anger right back at those with similar characteristics as they have. They've been conditioned by their experiences in this society to internalize their anger and redirect it at the most vulnerable target. It's not easy to direct this frustration and anger at the dominant members of society, so they direct it at each other. This sometimes makes members of one's own group difficult to get along with.

Many of the dominant members of society have been conditioned that Blacks are inferior. Most of its institutions and their leaders teach this. We have what is called institutional racism. These members learn to be prejudice, to discriminate, and to be bigoted. In this case it will be difficult to have a relationship with such individuals.

But not all of the dominant members of society internalize this bigotry, prejudice, and racism. Many of them can still see a person, regardless of color, religion, or ethnic origin, for what they're worth. They can evaluate you based upon your personality and who you are to them.

Many Blacks have a healthy, and positive regard for one another, in spite of the self-hate that's so rampant within Black culture.

These are the kind of people you want to have as your friends: those who can accept and have positive regard for you. Regardless of what their ethnic group is, if they put your best interest above all else, they will make good friends.

A good friend won't tell a joke at your expense, or make you the butt of any of his jokes. A good friend won't put you down to build himself up. A good friend won't offer you alcohol to the point of inebriation or saturation. A good friend won't get you involved in inappropriate activity of any kind. A good friend will look out for your interest and your welfare. A good friend won't play nasty tricks on you. A good friend won't play one friend against another. A good friend won't pretend to be your friend until a third party enters the picture then abandon you to the wolves. A good friend won't call you inappropriate names in front of his other friends. A good friend won't ask you to switch girls just when you are getting adjusted to the one you're with. A good friend won't always expect you to pay his way. A good friend won't always expect things to go his way, but will also act in your best interest.

Never let someone dominate you because you want them to be your friend. Don't do inappropriate things just to make someone your friend. Don't try and buy a friend—it never works. Don't agree with others just to encourage them to be your friend. Don't let a so-called friend abuse you for any reason: if they are truly a friend they won't try to abuse you. Don't volunteer to do something for a friend if it is beyond your capabilities: let your friends know what you will and won't do.

Don't choose your friends based upon their race, religion, or ethnic background; but choose them based upon their overall personalities—rather than a single factor in their personalities, and their demonstrated empathy, warmth, and concern for you as an individual.

Friendship is a mutual proposition, and all parties involved deserve reciprocal admiration and respect.

Be encouraged!!!!!!!!!!!!

October 14, 2009

8

Six Topics We Didn't Discuss

The reason I didn't talk to you about these topics is because I was hoping you'd figure them out for yourself, and hopefully you did. However, psychologists don't recommend letting children figure things out for themselves. They say children can't possibly figure out how to negotiate the world by themselves, they need guidance. They say you should let children know what your expectations are. Open, honest, and meaningful communication between parents and children about all subjects are recommended. I know it was wrong, but it was easier to let you figure them out for yourself. I was too lazy and uninvolved. I figured, why bother you if you were doing OK. But I really had no idea how you were doing. I hope by not talking to you about these topics you haven't experienced any unnecessary trauma.

I realize you're practically a grown man now, and talking to you about these topics might be coming somewhat late, but I decided to talk about them anyway. Saying something now is like closing the barn door after the horse has gone out to pasture. I hope some of it may not be too late to have a positive effect on you.

When I was growing up I had no one to talk to me about anything—for the most part. I roamed the hills and drowned myself in my own thoughts. I had to experience everything by trial and error—the hard way.

My brothers were in and out most of the time, and we never established any significant interpersonal communication. They had their own problems. My mother and I didn't have purposeful communication. Neither did I have any established communication with any of my sisters. My father was out of town most of the time, and we never established any special communication. There were no significant others that I could talk to about personal or general issues. As I got older I found myself having only superficial communication with those in my environment: we only talked about how to survive from day-to-day, not a deeper level of interpersonal communication. Because of my stuttering, even my family avoided communication with me whenever possible. There wasn't much opportunity for meaningful communication at school.

In most cases people move a great deal. We live in a highly mobile society. Most children aren't around their cousins, uncles, aunts, or grandparents. Parents are often the only ones to discuss interpersonal issues. In addition, in too many cases there's only one parent. If a parent doesn't let their child know what they expect, the child is likely to pick up bad habits in the streets. In this case the only ones they have to listen to are their peers. Teachers are about teaching, and not about helping students with personal issues. Counselors are too busy scheduling to do this kind of activity. Social workers usually are too busy with the more problem students.

There are six topics that I'd like to have discussed with you: money, religion, fighting, drugs and alcohol, sex, and school. We should have talked about many things, and had ongoing communication, but here's how I generally feel about these topics.

First, money—you shouldn't spend all your money on frivolous things. You should spend some and save some. One friend would say, "Don't spend what you don't have." If you don't make any money, don't spend any. This sounds simple, but it will keep your finances balanced. Always try to stay even. You don't need to spend all your money on the latest fashions; clothes don't determine who you are. Blacks spend too much of their money on their backs, and on what we drive. None of it lasts very long. Invest your money in something that'll last.

Many of us get too many credit cards and spend money we don't have. Make a habit not to loan money; people have a habit of not paying you back. Don't borrow money either, even if you have every intention of paying it back. There's a verse in the Bible that says, "Neither a borrower nor a lender be." You'll find that you won't get as angry with your friends if you don't loan to them or borrow from them.

Second, alcohol and drugs—never use drugs unless prescribed by a physicians, and don't use them then in a way to get addicted. It'll be tempting in college, because many of the kids will experiment with drugs, but always say no—no matter how down or depressed you feel. Some people will even use drugs to say, if you get high with me, we can do anything you like. Don't let them entice you.

It will be even more tempting to drink. Friends will say, "Everybody is doing it." Underage folks aren't supposed to drink at all. Sometimes people will even put some deleterious substance in your drink to achieve a desired effect. Save drinking for when you get to be of drinking age. At that point it's OK to take a social drink now and then.

Some people will try to get you drunk or high on drugs for the purpose of misusing you. Don't let that happen to you. I've seen people get taken advantage of sexually, or robbed, after becoming inebriated. Always try to stay in your right mind and conscious.

Third, religion—you need to go to church if you can. There're some good values being passed around in church. Of course, church people don't all have positive intentions. Some people believe in God, some don't; whatever you believe, church is a good place to be. Some people believe in a god, but don't believe in the Bible or traditional religion; some believe that all concepts of God are fallacious; others believe the Bible is the unadulterated word of God. As I've done with everything else, I'll leave it up to you to figure out what you believe in.

I personally believe man created God and religion because he needed something to believe in. The Bible has many good things to say, yet some of what it says isn't good for Black people. For example, the Bible indicates that Black people were condemned to a life of inferiority, because Ham's son saw him naked. There are other passages in the Bible that suggests Blacks be subservient. I believe there's a God-like force in the universe that keeps everything in balance. You can believe whatever your conscious dictates.

Fourth, school—I've said many things about school that I fear repeating myself. School is the foundation for the rest of your life. You need to study hard and make good grades. Good grades will be necessary if you want to go to the next level. Go to class, pay attention, and do your assignments. Get to class on time and don't fall asleep in class. Stay out of trouble by not doing anything foolish. Be careful who your friends are, sometimes friends can get you into trouble. Try to work out a balance between your schoolwork and your social life. Get involved in some extra-curricula activities. These activities should compliment your skills in a way to create a natural flow—not something that'll cause a strain on you.

Fifth, fighting—I don't think you have any problems in this area, at least none that I know about—that's good news. Some people who're small in stature have a complex, and are always picking fights, kind of like the neighborhood bully. Fighting can only lead to death, injury, or jail. Avoid fights whenever you can. It's always best to walk away from a fight—regardless of the situation. But never let anyone push you around. If you're in a group situation, people take cues from one another; if they see one person pushing you around, other of them will get into the act. Soon you'll be the scapegoat for the group. I realize that sometimes a fight is unavoidable. In that case give it all you've got. Just don't kill anyone.

Sixth, sex—sex is a very tricky subject. I deliberately made it the sixth topic. This subject is the one that most parents fear to discuss with their children. At one time things were different; today we're living in the twenty-first century. Naturally being a parent, I'd like to see you be a so-called "normal" heterosexual male. But some children prefer not to be in a heterosexual relationship, but prefer the same sex, for one reason or the other—usually because of childhood experiences. Every parent would like to have grandchildren. It's your life and you have to live it for yourself. Whatever you can live with. If you choose to be homosexual, you must be prepared for the ridicule and discrimination because of it—even today. You must be prepared to live with the consequences of your decision.

I hope you can profit by what I have to say. I know it's no substitute for early on-going communication. But I hope it's not too late for you to benefit. By now you have probably formed some deeply ingrained ideas. I only regret that we couldn't have discussed these topics earlier.

If you can use one point I have made here, it was worth it.

Be respectful!!!!!!!!!!!!!!!

October 21, 2009

9

Understanding Violence in the Black Community

A lot of talk has been going around recently concerning violence in the Black community. I wanted to present to you what I think are the reasons for this violence. The only reason I am presenting this point of view is because violence is likely to come up in some of your conversations. My view is somewhat radical, and you may or may not want to discuss my point of view in discussions around the campus. Your own point of view might be more appropriate. Sometimes it's even better to listen than to speak. However, there's always a right time to speak up.

I've discussed our history of slavery on many occasions in my various writings. Although, I'm sure you haven't read many of my writings. I believe that pre-slavery, slavery, post-slavery, and present-day experiences has contributed to our violent attitude. Our problems began over 10,000 years ago when other groups first set foot on the African continent. But more specifically, our violence stem from our conditioning during these periods. There are those who will say that some Blacks tend to blame everything on slavery. But slavery is the modern genesis experience for Blacks in the Western world.

We have been conditioned in many ways in this society. Our conditioning toward self-hate is the basis of our violent behavior. We were conditioned to dislike all of our characteristics: our hair, our noses, our skin color, our eyes, the size of our feet, our full–size buttocks. We were taught to feel inferior about all these qualities, and also about many aspects of our culture. This eventually turned to self-hate. If a person doesn't like himself he will not like those who look like him. We therefore turn our self-hate on those who look like us. We take all the negativity directed toward us and redirect it toward each other.

Part of the reason we do this is because those responsible for our victimization don't make easily accessible targets. We have all this frustration, and no one to direct it toward except each other; most of the time we're the ones who live in proximity to one another. Those who're most likely to commit such violence are likely to be overcrowded in poverty areas where there's a great deal of frustrations. We take our frustrations and direct them toward our family, neighbors, and anyone who looks like us; because it's us that we hate.

The criminal justice system plays another trick on us. In addition to us being packed in ghettos among each other, we get a heavier sentence for killing someone white than for killing another Black person. Throughout history the penalty for killing a Black man has been rather light, and rather high for killing a white man. So if we kill someone they're more likely to be Black. We're conditioned that way by the system.

We have existed in a pressure cooker in the cities for a long period of time. Social scientists say if such conditions are allowed to build for a long period of time they're likely to exponentially increase, not just increase but multiply the same way rats multiply. That explains why we're beginning to see such an increase in problems in the Black community. The problems have reached a boiling point and are ready to explode. The more unstable conditions are over a period of time the more explosive they become.

Some say our history isn't responsible for our current level of violence. If our history is responsible, why was there less violence a number of years ago? Because we're experiencing times that are breaking the camel's back. Everything has a final breaking point.

Social conditions are similar to weather conditions: if you get certain patterns existing in the atmosphere over a period of time you'll get a definite set of weather conditions. By the same token, if you get certain social patterns existing over a period of time you'll get certain definite social conditions.

Some of these negative social conditions include lack of adequate education, unemployment, lack of housing, political disfranchisement, and family disruption. Such social conditions create a cancer that feeds on itself. Young men without jobs or hopes for a better future overcrowd in the ghetto. The only viable jobs become selling drugs and other underground illegal activities. Their lives become focused on gang activity, and killing one another to protect their turf. The answers to their problem seemingly become self and other destruction. It's all they can see for their future.

I know many won't concur with my understanding of violence in the Black community. Some will even go as far as saying there's something inherent in the genes of Blacks causing them to behave as they do. At this point it'll do no good to argue with them. Healthy debate is a whole different situation.

Be gracious!!!!!!!!!!!!

October 28, 2009

10

Take Your Time

Be satisfied with where you are at any particular place in time. Don't get worried about your next move, or where you could be, to the extent that you don't take advantage of where you are now. Take it slow you've got plenty of time.

When I was in high school I couldn't wait to get out of high school, and move on to college. I was cognizant of the fact that I had wasted a lot of time in elementary, junior, and high school. I spent a lot of time thinking about what I'd do beyond high school. I should've focused on high school and making the best of where I was. There was plenty of time to think about and cxperience college.

When I was in college I kept feeling I was missing something by being in the dorm room studying all the time. I felt like I was missing all the fun and action with the girls. In spite of the fact it was my choice to be there, and I wanted to be there. I felt pressure to be making relationships and getting on with my life. There was really nothing better to do with this stage of my life but to be in college, studying, and preparing for my future. I had a lot of anxiety and pressure because I wasn't satisfied with myself or my background. I felt the need to always be on the move. My background had given me a lot of emotional turmoil and internal conflicts.

Don't ever feel the pressure to be doing something else; be satisfied with what you're doing at the present time. Take care of that and you can move on to the next stage at the appropriate time. There's nothing better you could be doing at the present time than getting your education. You have everything you need right there on campus. Take advantage of it instead of idealizing being someplace else, and seeing that other place as being better than where you are.

When I graduated I went into the military. The reason I went into the military was because when I graduated I didn't feel comfortable with where I was. I left school prematurely because I was in such a hurry to move on with my life, even though I had received my degree. I didn't have a car to transport myself, and my folks lived way back off the beaten path. It would have been impossible for me to get around back in those woods. None of my brothers or sisters offered me the opportunity to live with them until I could get on my feet. I had no cash to help me get started. The only option I could see was to join the military.

Even when I joined the military, I joined of my own free will, but soon became dissatisfied. I worried myself into a frenzy being concerned about what I could have been doing had I not joined the military. I put a lot of pressure on myself because I was dissatisfied with my station in life. I worried about such things as a house, a car, and clothes. One of my reasons for joining the military was because I didn't want to get hung up with paying for an apartment, a car, and buying clothes. These things to me didn't seem meaningful before joining the military.

Again, in the military I worried about having relationships. When I first joined the military we had to be on base ten weeks before getting leave. The only women we saw were the few women on the base. I wasn't somehow satisfied with my ability to get into and maintain relationships. I should have been satisfied with playing games and socializing on the base. Instead, I ran around like a chicken with its head cut off, desperate to find relationships.

When I got out of the military I finally realized that I had to somehow relax and get rid of all the pressure and anxiety. There was nothing to be in a hurry for, no place to be in a hurry to get to. I think you'll find this true at most periods of your life.

One of the best things you can do in this life is to learn to be satisfied and comfortable with whatever position you find yourself. And I hope you are comfortable being in college, and don't find yourself under a lot of pressure or anxiety to be doing something else. Learn to make the best of your present situation.

So take it easy and enjoy every stage of your life. If you are stuck in the dorm, take it easy and play cards, video games, learn to play pool in the recreation room, or just kick it with your friends. You can always sit back and read a good book. I had too much anxiety to sit down and play games or read a good book; I had to be on the move. Even when I studied my mind wasn't really on it.

Enjoy, right now! There is nothing for you to do but to enjoy college. There is no place to rush to or to get to, nothing you could better be doing. Make the most of your time in college. That means balancing your time between your studies, school activities, and your social life. You probably already know this. I am telling you because apparently at your age I didn't have enough sense to realize it.

Be judicious!!!!!!

November 4, 2009

11

Still Nervous After All These Years

I want to tell you a story, and I'm going to tell it like it is. I've told you some aspects of this story before in one of my emails, but it bears repeating. I can't stress too much where I came from. I was born in the middle of nowhere. There was only a three-mile trail to my house. This trail led off a winding, hilly, blacktopped road that led to small towns in either direction. The town to the south was twenty miles away and was about 45,000. The town to the north was twenty miles away and it was approximately 2,000. Ten miles further to the north was a town of approximately 100,000.

We lived on a fifty-acre-dirt farm. We raised a few animals, grew food to feed them, as well as food to feed ourselves. But what I want to get across is the isolation in which I grew up. We didn't get a graded-dirt road until I was seven-years old. Until that time few people dared to venture back that far off the beaten path. Only a horse or a wagon could negotiate this trail. Any traveler had to braze the dew, the streams, the tree limbs, the mud, and the deep trenches. Most souls weren't brave enough to travel back that far. Sometimes I don't understand how they hauled the recycled lumber through those woods to even build the rusty, tin-roof, shotgun shack. My parents didn't seem to think anything of this isolation.

I didn't start to school until I was almost seven-years old. In that school district if your birthday came after September you had to wait until the next year. When I did enter school I went to a segregated school. It was that way throughout elementary, junior, and high school, and I have existed in segregated situations for most of my life.

There was only one restaurant in the small town where our school was located. It was segregated with a small room set up in the back for Blacks. This room was unpainted and had the smell of mildew. The few tables and chairs in it were broken-down castoffs from the white section. Segregation was at its highest form. The facilities in towns nearby were also segregated. The theatres, clubs, and organizations were all segregated.

When I graduated from high school, I thought I was ready for the world, but I found out I had a lot of learning to do. My brother had bought me a car, but it was getting in disrepair, and I didn't feel I would have time to care for it in college. I left for Houston one Saturday night to take it back to my brother. If I had been thinking I would have gotten my father to trade it in on something better. But I wanted to settle down and be serious about my studies—not waste time with an old car. On my way to Houston I got sleepy, and stopped at a small, run-down highway café, as a person normally would do.

"Go to the back," the manager said, "Around back is where we serve colored customers."

I went back, had a good look at where he was directing me, and came back up front. The area was unpainted, had broken-down furniture, and some of the windows were broken. I thought times had changed. This was 1966.

"What do you mean go back there?" I asked.

"If you don't get out of here, you'll find out what I mean," he said.

"Well, if you feel that way about it, I don't want anything from here anyway."

I was at first determined to get service.

"Nigger, get out of here."

I could feel myself getting angry, and thought I better leave before one of us do something we'd be sorry for. I realized then that noting had changed, especially in that part of Texas. The situation at the café was a quick initiation into the big world. It signified to me that I was all grown up now, and that I should get ready to take my punishment.

When I entered college I'm not sure what I expected. But I thought it would be better than where I was getting away from. I chose the college because it wasn't too far from my home, and I could always travel back and forth on holidays. I knew very little about the college, and should have been trying to get much farther away.

The school maintained many old Southern traditions, these traditions were apparent to anyone visiting the campus. The whole campus had a general discriminatory atmosphere. Blacks were not encouraged to join fraternities, clubs, or other organizations. Socially it was for most purposes segregated. Black and white students attending sporting events sat in different sections of whatever the arena, even though Blacks participated on the teams.

I never got over my feelings of isolation, or improved in my socialization. Sometimes in class when the professor asked me a question, I would be shaking in my boots. Sometimes even just sitting in class I would be nervous. I had always been a little nervous. I'm not sure if that is genetic, or if it comes from being isolated in those woods for so many years. I must admit that sometimes I acted more like a caged animal. I developed the instincts of a coyote after being in those woods and not being around many people.

I was frustrated and generally had a certain amount of anxiety. Some of the teachers made me feel uncomfortable by obviously discriminating in some ways. I even isolated myself from most of the Black students, and spent most of my time studying. Teachers, students, and staff treated me as if I was invisible, as Ralph Ellison suggests in his novel, *The*

Invisible Man. All these things and others conspired to make me feel uncomfortable on campus.

On one occasion an English professor suggested that Othello wasn't Black, but was a Moor; and consequently no miscegenation was involved in his relationship with Desdemona. That made their relationship acceptable. On another occasion an English professor encouraged a Chinese student to sit up front when the Chinese student and I sat in back of the class. He left me sitting in back with no such encouragement. He did at least give me a passing grade in the course. In a sociology class the professor reminded the class that all groups had the same innate level of intelligence. One white female wanted to know it those tall Watusi had the same level of intelligence as other groups.

The boys in my dorm decided to organize a panty raid. We organized a group and left the boys' dorm headed for one of the girls' dorm. The boys were frenetic, "Panty raid!" they screamed. One student from another dorm saw some Blacks in the crowd, and yelled out, "Blacks can't get white panties!" I stopped, like a deer caught in the headlights of an oncoming car. I was embarrassed and left the group and returned to my dorm. I had never been so humiliated and mortified. Knowing that I wanted any sex with a female I could get.

I had many tense moments where I stayed on edge. Psychologists say when individuals are constantly under tension, they can release emotional toxins in the form of hormones into their system, which can affect their entire system and cause some emotional or psychiatric problems. Keep in mind that I was maladjusted when I went to college. I wasn't comfortable around people in general. Some of my problems were social, and no one reached out and addressed those needs.

This is why I encouraged you to attend a Black university, but I guess you had to face the real world sooner or later. I felt you would have a better chance of getting some kind of a degree, and a better chance of advancing to the next educational level. You might have had a better opportunity to develop socially as well. I have always been a little distrustful of whites, based on the way they have treated me over the years, and my observations of how they treat Black people in general. I really didn't want to turn my last son over to them, knowing how unfair they can be. Although, I realize that part of my problem was because of where I came from. I was just a jungle boy.

I know white people have the same fears, shed the same tears and die in so many years. They also bleed when cut; fall down when knocked off balance; and die when they receive sufficient trauma to the body. But I guess my feelings come from all those years of conditioning as a child. Conditioning is a hell of a thing, and is difficult to overcome, once it has been reinforced on a daily basis.

I still get a little nervous around a bunch of strange white people—especially, and around some Black people as well. I guess I've read about, seen, and experienced too much negative treatment toward Blacks on the part of whites. I never know what to expect from them.

Life is to be enjoyed, not full of stress and anxiety. Don't let any situation give you anxiety.

Never Give up, remain steadfast!!!!!!!!!!!!!

November 11, 2009

12

Don't Be Satisfied With a Limited Education

I grew up without my parents or other family members involving me in any pre-school educational activities. I didn't even know colors, sizes, geometric shapes, or the alphabet. There was a lot I didn't know that I should have known as a first-grade student. I didn't have the benefit of pre-kindergarten, kindergarten, day-care, or head start. I also had a severe stuttering problem. To top that off I was isolated along a three-mile trail that led off the main road. This trail was navigable only by horse and wagon. Few souls were brave enough to venture that far off the beaten path to our house.

I didn't start to school until I was almost seven. In that district if your birthday came after September you had to wait until the next year to enter school. My parents didn't feel comfortable enough with their own education to help me with mine. We had no electricity, gas, indoor plumbing, or telephone.

I did fairly well my first several years in school. If you consider that even then no one paid me much attention. I was simply there to learn what I could through listening to the teachers, there were no hands on. I never did get any special attention. No one even showed me how to do such a simple task as how to form my letters.

In the sixth grade my teacher was the band director. He had to teach sixth grade and somehow manage the band activities. He was not good at doing either. Once he asked us to do an assignment, and I picked a piece of paper from the floor and turned it in. He put a grade on the paper and a grade in his grade book. It was the only assignment I remember doing during this and the next year. I lost a lot of ground during these two years. I guess the school district was too cheap to hire a band director and a sixth-grade teacher.

In the seventh grade I was unlucky enough to get the same band director. That year they switched him to seventh grade. I was exempt from several classes to spend time with the band director in the band room. I spent too much time during these years following the band director around, when I should have been in class. I didn't know any better. I thought I was getting away with something; instead I was scamming myself out of an education. In addition, the band director made no attempt to teach me how to read music. I had never had as much as a toy instrument, and didn't know enough about music to teach myself. There were no fundamentals of music education in our school. The band director was satisfied to have me sit there making foul notes, and being a body in the marching band. I quit the band in the eighth grade. I figured if I couldn't read music I was wasting my time.

My class was divided into two sections throughout my school years. There were approximately eighty students in the whole class. I believe the class was later divided according to those who had promise and those who had no promise. My section was treated as if they had no promise. We spent too much time doing absolutely nothing. Of course, the children didn't mind. If you give children the option of doing nothing, they will opt to do nothing. I actually believe that the other class got a little more instruction than my class did. We were the second class, and I suppose the teachers got bored with repeating themselves.

In school we wrote few papers, read few novels, and went on few field trips. Our library was inadequate, and there was no library in that small town. I don't know today if the libraries in small towns nearby were open to Blacks, I never tried to enter any of them. In addition, there were no bookstores in the immediate area. We had too much down-time in which we just sat and stared out the window.

So I kept going until I graduated, mainly because I didn't know how much I didn't know. I badly wanted to change schools, but there was no way to change schools unless we moved, and we weren't about to do that. I had already wasted too much time in my present situation.

I knew I wanted to attend college, because I didn't want to be like some of my brothers, having to take undesirable jobs, when even they were available. I figured if I could get in college and get a degree I could be in line for a better job. I also had heard some of the more intelligent students say they were going to college. My cousin was a teacher at the high school, and I saw him as a role model.

I knew Social Security would give me a stipend if I kept going to school. The Balance in the Universe was in my favor in that regard. My father had retired when I was a sophomore, and I had gotten a monthly stipend ever since. I also was able to get a loan to cover the cost of my room and board as well as tuition. I had very little left after paying these fees, but was able to make it.

I attended a traditionally white Southern university, and this was apparent to anyone who came on the campus. They maintained a lot of the old Southern traditions. I was a bit nervous and anxious in some situations, but I was able to get a degree. While in college I always felt behind the eight ball, but I kept trying. In some situations I was out classed, but that only made me strive harder. When I graduated I wanted to go on to graduate school, but my funds were low. My help from Social Security ran out on my 23rd birthday. I decided to go into the Army instead.

If I made it with my background, there is certainly hope for you. The Balance in the Universe was seemingly always in my favor. I am lucky to have completed elementary school; lucky to have completed junior high; and lucky to have gotten a high school diploma. I am also lucky to have graduated college; lucky to have gotten two graduate degrees; and lucky to have worked on a Ph.D. at two Midwestern universities.

You have had better opportunities than I had; although, we all have different circumstances. So don't be satisfied with a limited education. Work hard and be courageous, doggedly determined, and tireless in your efforts to get an education.

Be thorough and persistent!!!!!!!!!!

November 18, 2009

13

Smarter or Work Harder?

Don't even give it a second thought that individuals from other groups are generally more intelligent than you: for example whites, Asians, etc. No one group is more intelligent than another group as a whole. Some individuals within each of these groups may be more intelligent. It's like one gunfighter said on one of my favorite cowboy TV shows, "There is always somebody a little bit faster and some a little bit slower than you are." In this case, there may be some people out there more intelligent than you are. Blacks have been led to believe, because of their history and what they've been unable to accomplish around the world, that some other groups are just more intelligent. Every group has an equal distribution of the highly intelligent, those who are medium range in intelligence, and those who are of low intelligence. All groups have an equal distribution of intellect. Individuals are simply sometimes afforded differential opportunities.

Asians generally come from strong families, they work hard, and a large number are at least of average intelligence. Those of average intelligence are the largest number within any group. Because they come from strong families and work hard generally cause them to be high achievers. But not all of them are intelligent. It just seems that way because they make use of every bit of potential they have in each individual within the community. They're trained this way.

In addition, Asians haven't had to contend with inferior schools, family disruption, a history of blatant discrimination and oppression to the same degree as Blacks. They also have not suffered the same political, economic, or educational oppression. Because of their family structure and their work ethic they've always been seen as high achievers.

Asians know they're coming from behind the eight ball, so they come out shooting straight from both hips. They put every bit of possible effort into their academic and work life. They aren't any smarter they just work harder.

I've heard of Asian students having to be told by their parents to go to bed at night, they were so absorbed in doing their homework. Some other groups don't want to spend even a few hours set up as a requirement for study. When they study a subject they study it from bottom to top. They look at it from every aspect and every angle. So at test time they're better prepared to master the test. Others simply give the material a cursory overview.

Nobody has to convince them to study, they're conditioned by their parents at an early age to study and do their homework, and to be observant and pay attention in class. They are conditioned that a good education is necessary for each individual in order to have a healthy well functioning, and well ordered society.

Whites have always had privilege in this society. They work hard, but often not as hard as Asians. Many of them simply don't feel they should have to work as hard. They feel opportunity in America is their birthright. Whites are more established in the norms and values of the country, and feel they should have rights whether they work hard or not. They just do what comes natural without expending a great deal of effort. Consequently, Asians sometimes outdo them.

Because Blacks have been oppressed, discriminated against, and kept in the ghetto in many instances for many years, they've been seen as low achievers. They've accepted the idea that they cannot achieve to the same degree as other groups, and are less intelligent. Blacks haven't been allowed to develop economically, politically, or educationally. Slavery and events prior to slavery almost destroyed their concept of family, economic stability, educational attainment, and manhood.

When you meet an Asians in school you meet someone who has been afforded many opportunities to be the best he can be. In addition, he has worked hard, and is also at least of average intelligence. He will seem super intelligent. He is probably no more intelligent than you are.

When you meet the average white student you will meet someone who has had every advantage. He will seem superior, but is probably no more intelligent than you are. He just has had every advantage in every way you can name. He usually has not had to work as hard as everyone else to achieve similar benefits.

There are still a lot of people who don't believe that Blacks are as capable as other groups. Richard J. Herrnstein and Charles Murray suggest the notion of Black inferiority in their book, *Bell* Curve (1994). Arthur Jensen suggests such a notion in an article in the *Harvard Educational Review* (1969). There has been any number of social scientists throughout history who has put forth the notion that Blacks are generally less intelligent. But most reputable social scientists and others generally tell us that all groups are equally capable. It's their history, economic opportunities, social opportunities, and educational opportunities that make the difference in their present-day performance.

In the Black family and community this notion of being inferior has gotten transmitted from one generation to another, to the extent that Blacks are almost convinced that members of their own group are less intelligent than those of other groups. Blacks kill each other; fail to cooperate with one another; not because of their intelligence, but mainly because of their societal conditioning. They also congregate in ghettos because of a lack of other opportunities. By telling a group that they're inferior for many years, and treating them as if they're inferior, it's enough to cause them to behave in an inferior manner. After so long you start to believe both you and your group are inferior.

You must get use to spending time in the library, doing your homework, working on projects and papers, looking at CNN, reading *Newsweek*, reading the local and national newspapers when possible, and otherwise concentrating on your studies. We know that most students don't work as hard as they should in high school. You have to be willing to commit to upgrading your study habits and techniques from high school. Studying is something that must be a part of you, or you will find it difficult to do. You must make an effort to have it become a part of you. In other words you must feel comfortable studying. When you sit down to study you must not have something else on your mind competing for your attention. You must make studying as natural as eating a bowl of cereal for breakfast.

If you apply yourself you can equal or do better than that Asian or white student. You must be resigned to work as hard as that Asian student, or that white student who has always known privilege. So don't let anyone convince you that you are less intelligent or less capable than anyone else. You can accomplish whatever you want if you came from a decent background, work hard, and are at least of average intelligence.

Be a hard worker!!!!!!!!!!

November 25, 2009

14

I've Been Jacked by Them All

Some people feel that only certain groups are going to hoodwink, bamboozle, or run them amuck; depending on their experiences with people. We should know by now that some people in every group will try to do this to you. It's in some people's nature to do this. It's not germane to any particular group, but is an individual thing.

Many people will try to hoodwink you if you come across to them in a certain manner. Even those who wouldn't ordinarily try to misuse you will do so, if you come across as vulnerable. People will generally first evaluate your behavior, and then set their agenda in regard to you. Again, it depends on how you respond to this agenda as to whether they continue to launch their program. Some say it's only human nature for people to respond in this manner.

Even if it's not in our human nature, it may be in our animal nature to try and run others amuck. We haven't always been so civilized. It seems that some residuals from our primitive nature carries over to modern times, and are still with us today. Such games as one-upmanship may still be written in our DNA. Also, do others before they do you, and always maintain the upper hand. As well as, stay on top of the game. Such things may still motivate us, and be part of our nature.

I have been jacked by the best of them: Northerners, Southerners, Westerners, and Easterners; African-Americans, European Americans, Chinese, Japanese, Vietnamese, Arabs, Indians, Mexicans, and others; educated and uneducated; rich and poor. It doesn't take a particular group to bamboozle you. We live in a society where we've been dominated by European-Americans. We sometimes get the idea that European-Americans are to blame for all of our problems.

It's not only European-Americans that discriminate against us. Some other groups will discriminate against us as quickly as European-Americans. It's some of these other group's participation that has allowed prejudice and bigotry to continue. Black people will even discriminate against each other for no valid reason. Blacks around the world will frequently discriminate against each other because of their conditioning by other groups, and their exposure to colonialism. Blacks were conditioned to self-hate which resulted in them disliking one another. Some groups who have been discriminated against as much as African-Americans will impose this same negativity on African-Americans. Somehow they feel a need to rise over African-Americans and keep them on the bottom.

Some people are in-group conscious. If you don't belong to their group then they feel you don't deserve any specials breaks. Being in-group conscious is not common among African-Americans; consequently, they discriminate against each other. In some cases they're more favorably disposed to other groups. African-Americans have been conditioned to self-hate, and disorganized so much that they've lost much of their sense of in-group consciousness.

Many African-Americans haven't learned to have love, trust, respect, unity, loyalty, or to consolidate our resources. This sometimes leaves us out in the cold when it comes to protection of one another, and being able to act collectively. Sometimes we fail to stand up for one another.

If you look at recorded history you'll see that most groups have taken advantage of other groups when it was convenient. Many groups participated in the slave trade, and have been responsible for negative actions against African-Americans. It has been said that slavery was strictly an economic proposition, and everyone who was allowed participated in it. Discrimination against African-Americans still has economic consequences, and is motivated for economic reasons. In that case many other groups see it as advantageous to keep African-Americans at a lower level of the economy.

Arabs were some of the first to participate in the slave trade. Some people who have darker skin than some African-Americans still feel an obligation to discriminate against them. One group will take advantage of another as long as there's economic benefit in them doing so. Some groups feel they have to keep other groups at a disadvantage.

Discrimination between people can occur for many reasons: ethnic differences, religious differences, skin color, etc. People discriminate for many foolish reasons: such as the people in the conflict in Rwanda, the conflict in Bosnia, and I understand the Japanese have long-standing conflicts with the Koreans. I'm sure we'll never fully understand some of the subtleties involved in why one group discriminates against another. It's felt that a group will find some reasons to discriminate. If it's not skin color it will be hair color, eye color, texture of hair, foot size, or even height. It's comforting for some groups to feel they're somehow better than another.

We must learn to be good judges of character, and see people for what they bring to the table. We live in a multi-ethnic, multi-cultural society, and can't afford to judge people based on so-called race, religion, or ethnic considerations; as many of us try to do. It's time to judge people based on the content of their character.

If anybody tells you something different than what I say in these emails, they don't have your best interest at heart. Some people will tell you things aren't really this way, but when you examine things closely for yourself, you'll find them to be exactly this way.

Be discerning!!!!!!!!!!!

December 2, 2009

15

Don't Party Like it's 1999

There was a song out in the 1960s or 1970s mentioning something about "Partying like it was 1999." To me that insinuated partying like it was late in the season. I could be wrong in my assumption.

During this period young people were using drugs and alcohol to get high and party, even more so than usual. But there was no reason then or now to party like the world is coming to an end. People have always felt the world was coming to an end, and that we were in the end times of the world. Whatever the situation, it's best to keep things in moderation.

Plato in 300 B.C. spoke of the world as coming to an end, there was too much corruption, and the world had reached a critical period in world history where it was reaching the end of time. There was too much negativity in the world. In other words, the world was going to hell in a hand basket—even then.

Ministers and others presently talk about us having arrived at a time of famine, disease, pestilence, wars, and rumors of wars; a time spoken of in the Bible as the rapture and Armageddon—soon to appear.

Others have talked throughout history about the world coming to an end, but it hasn't ended yet. People mention prostitution, drug abuse, homosexuality, and murder, as a sign that we're reaching end times; but these things have always been around.

There's no need to party like the world will soon end. I guarantee you that unless someone releases an atom or hydrogen bomb, the world will be around for a long time, and will go on as usual. There's no reason to believe that world leaders are unintelligent enough to release such a bomb. Years from now people will speak about how those of our period thought the world was coming to an end, but if didn't.

Instead of partying like it is 1999; you as a young adult should be spending this time getting yourself together, getting your education, getting your social life and your personal life together, and preparing for your future. Live as if there's nothing but hope for the future, because you should have nothing but hope for your future. Such an attitude could change the whole world, if enough felt that way. If you live this way you'll find yourself enjoying life more.

I personally believe you have a bright future ahead of you. I know that saying people have a bright future has become a cliché, but I definitely mean it. I say it has become cliché, because when I was working at a mental health center, several patients who had been admitted over 100 times, said while they were being discharged, "I have a bright future." I've also heard a number of other people use it as cliché. I don't make a habit of using these words. But in any case, don't let people sidetrack you into making your life one big party.

Be sure you study when you should, and socialize in your spare time—not the opposite. The rest will take care of itself. Don't forget what I said, "Do the best you can, and to hell with the rest." I know I've stated this several times.

The world is going to go on, and we're going to keep living like we always have. So spend your time preparing yourself for living—not for death. Preparing for death is not a worthwhile activity. Some ministers seemingly try to get you to prepare for death.

Don't listen to anyone who says, you may as well enjoy yourself, because we don't have much time left on earth.

Some people will give as a reason for drinking and using drugs, that everybody's doing it, but that's no reason to ruin your life, because everybody's doing it.

As I'm sitting here, I'm looking at a movie on "TVOne" called "Last Stand." It's about a young man who thought he knew everything, wouldn't listen to his father. He got involved in drugs and alcohol in high school but kicked it. He left home and went to Hollywood with big dreams of being a standup comedian. He got under a lot of pressure, and went back to drugs and alcohol, after a friend encourage him to try some of his stash. I didn't finish seeing the movie, because Frances came in and changed the channel. It simply demonstrated how young Black men go wrong.

Stay away from drugs and alcohol; they can ruin your life. If you drink anything, be sure you at least stay sober enough to know what you're doing. If you're drinking be sure you hold on to your drink, don't give anyone an opportunity to put a foreign substance in it. And always know exactly what you're drinking.

Be sober!

December 9, 2009

16

Developing Social and Communication Skills

Learn to work closely and cooperate with other people in group settings. The whole world has moved toward a team concept—especially most corporations. Those who can't function in a team concept will be lost in a modern technological society.

It requires social and communication skills to function in a team concept. I never developed the social skills to function in group settings. Consequently, I had problems in my work settings with relating to people.

When I grew up I was isolated at the end of a three-mile trail. There was no graded or paved road to my house. Not many people ventured back that far off the beaten path. My speech never developed as it should have, because not only did we get few visitors, but my family members rarely talked to me. When I got to school my speech impediment affected my ability to develop social skills. But I stumbled and mumbled on through.

I never had many friends, and when I did it was always one-on-one, never group oriented. Consequently, I had difficulty functioning in groups, but can manage to handle myself in a one-on-one situation.

In college there weren't many opportunities to function in group settings, and I spent most of my time in my room reading. I still didn't improve in my speech or social skills. I should have at least minored in speech, and attempted to be a bit more social. I didn't know all this when I went to college. I thought I could isolate myself, read my books, not keep up with current events, and everything would be fine. I was totally wrong.

So when I got into the workplace, I vastly lacked social skills. I hope you never have such issues to deal with. You weren't as isolated as I was, and have been in groups all your life. This should work to your benefit.

That's why you shouldn't isolate yourself; stay involved with people, and try to get along with them. I never learned the normal give and take involved in relationships, and I never felt comfortable working in group settings.

Take some courses in speech if you can. Speech will help to prevent there being any impediments to your communicating, and help to facilitate this communication. If you can't function in a group, naturally you're going to be at a disadvantage.

You need to keep up with what's going on in the world so you cannot only participate in classroom discussions, but tie what you read in with classroom discussions. Keeping up with current events will also facilitate conversations with friends. Some professors will throw in a question about current events on their test, depending on whether the event is related to the course. So it's important to keep up with current events.

In addition there were so many general things about life that I should have known that I had no conception of. I call it being under-socialized, and not being familiar with the ways of mainstream culture. There were so many things I missed while growing up, being limited culturally.

Take a job today and the first thing they do is send you through training that's designed to get you to learn to function as a team member. Understanding and being able to function in a team concept is almost as important as your degree.

The only reason I made it through high school, college, and graduate school, is because I was headstrong and didn't pay anybody any attention. I was only concerned about my own objectives. Now that's one way, but I wouldn't recommend doing it that way. The world has changed since I was in school. You should be involved with those around you, to the degree that you can.

Anything you do requires the ability to communicate well. People judge you by your ability to communicate. Take it from someone who could have been more successful at his career had he taken the time to develop his ability to communicate. Social skills and ability to communicate are somehow interconnected, so that one enhances the other. Both social skills and communication are important for functioning in a team concept.

I think you'll find especially in public relations that speech is very important. Some fields require excellent communication skills. If you're going to create images for people, you need to have a good image yourself. Good communication skills should be part of that image. But don't worry you have plenty of time to develop good communication skills. Remember, developing such skills require effort and hard work; no one is born with these skills.

Until next time, stay strong!

December 16, 2009

17

Why Study Speech?

When you were in high school I suggested you take a speech course. I didn't suggest it because your speech was poor, but because everyone should take speech. It's basic to any high school curriculum, and I noticed you were beginning to mumble and chew your words—trying to be hip like some of the other teenagers. You said they didn't have a speech course in your curriculum. I didn't follow up on it because I wanted it to be your decision, and didn't want to put pressure on you. But I found it hard to believe your high school didn't have a speech course.

My reason for suggesting it was because no matter how good your speech, a speech course could only improve your speech. We live in a highly technological and fast–pace society. One's speech is very important. In most cases people judge you by the way you talk. It's one of the few ways they have for judging and making decisions about you. Some other groups have a general stereotype of Black people who come in mumbling and generally being inarticulate. If you don't make a good impression with your speech, you are almost lost. It's sometimes even more important than the way you dress, though your manner of dress is also important.

I feel that if there is any way you can squeeze some speech courses into your college curriculum, I would suggest you do so. I realize your curriculum is already designed for you, but such electives in speech as Introduction, Voice and Diction, Debate, and some others would help you to make a better presentation once you do get your degree. Not only in terms of presentation, but there are lots of reasons for being able to communicate more effectively. I say this for several reasons, mostly because of my own experiences.

To begin with, I developed a habit of stuttering in my childhood. I don't know if it was genetic or developed out of my environmental situation. But I lived at the end of a three-mile trail. There was no road to my house until I was in the first grade. Only a wagon or horse could negotiate that trail. The trail led to a narrow, winding, hill-ridden, blacktopped highway that led into small cities: one 20 miles to the north (2,000 in population), and another 20 miles to the south (45,000 in population). Few people came by to visit us, which meant limited contact with people outside the family. To top that off my family members had very little to say to me.

People had the habit of asking my relatives questions about me rather than talking to me directly. My father took a job on the Gulf Coast and spent little time at home. When I grew up there was no one but my sister and mother to talk to, and I had too much work on the farm to do rather than spend time talking with them. I spent most of my time doing chores. There was little time for socialization. Consequently, my socialization skills and speech skills were underdeveloped. My father later would have me drive him places, but he always had me to stay in the car while he went inside to visit. This further handicapped my socialization and speech skills.

In school there was no such thing as speech therapy. We didn't have a speech therapist for miles around. My parents didn't even have transportation into the city for any such thing as speech therapy, nor the funds to pay for it. We were mostly concerned with the basics: food, clothing and shelter. We barely had the basics. So I stumbled through school as best I could, with my terrible stuttering habit. But I was determined to go to college. Even with my speech problem, I knew I was a fairly intelligent guy, though some people treated me as if I was retarded.

If I had to go through college again, the one thing I would do is take more speech courses. I have two Master's degrees, and worked on a Ph.D. at two different universities. But I needed to work more on my speech, for my speech is still deficient in some ways.

I feel I have been rejected because of this one basic issue on many occasions—both socially and vocationally. Even when I was able to get a job, my speech was instrumental in preventing me from being able to rise in the organization, and maintaining that employment situation.

These are the reasons I keep suggesting to you that you take some speech courses. I know there's nothing wrong with your speech, aside from you trying to talk like most teenagers. But if you can find room for several elective speech courses, I promise you will not regret it. I don't want you to be like that proverbial ape, but to profit from my mistakes, and not have to engage in so much trial-and-error learning.

One man said once that, "Presentation is everything." I believe this to be the case. If you are dressed well, have good hygiene, and articulate well, you're likely to make a good impression. If these things are true for you, in most cases, you're likely to make a good presentation. Isn't that your objective!

Be intense!!!!!!!!!!!!

December 23, 2009

18

The Importance of Speaking, Reading, and Writing Effectively

Speaking, reading, and writing are basic to a good education. If you're going to get very far educationally, vocationally, or otherwise; it's good to have a command of all three of these areas. In fact, a higher level of education is not recommended by high school counselors and teachers unless you have good facility with all three. They would encourage a vocational school instead of going to college—especially if you haven't mastered the basics.

Speaking is important because people judge you based on the way you speak. It's good to be able to communicate well. Presentation is very important in this society. I have been, and have seen a lot of people rejected because of their inability to communicate fluently. If you can't speak well it'll be difficult to get the undivided attention of a group or individual. The better you can speak, other things being equal, the more successful you can be. That's why I keep suggesting that you take all the elective speech courses you can. If you can't speak fluently everybody seems to ignore you, or just don't want to be bothered. If you plan to spend your life on the corner with the fellows, then maybe good speech isn't necessary.

You must be able to read at an acceptable level to do well in any subject. And the educational system requires you to be able to respond in writing to what you read. Then you must be able to explain what you've read. Two people can get different meaning from a book, but there should be a general range of meaning. Literature has different interpretations to different people, depending on their backgrounds.

The more you read the more knowledgeable you'll become—in most situations, and the further you can go in the educational system. You'll continue to add to your knowledge throughout life as you read. If you can't read you won't get far. Reading gives you pleasure, and allows you to explore the society around you. You'll find rhythm and beauty in language. You can't read a book once, and feel that you are familiar with it. You must at least read for a second time. The First time you read is to get a broad understanding; the second time is for getting a handle on the details.

Writing is where reading and speaking comes together. Chances are if you can read and speak well you can write well. There's normally a relationship between speaking, reading, and writing. The only way to learn to write is to sit in the chair and practice. Your style and your approach to writing are your own.

Writing is mostly revision. One should never think they can write a good paper or article by giving it the once over. That is to write it, turn it in, and forget it. It's taxing, but one should read the paper over and over, as many times as it takes to rid the paper of all its mistakes. Let a friend or someone else read over the paper to be sure there are no glaring mistakes. It's hard for an individual to proofread his own work. Don't completely rely on your spell and grammar check either. Remember in writing your job is to bring black marks to life, and how you do that depends on who you are.

I hope you're better at speaking, reading, and writing than I was at your age. I had difficulty doing all three. No one seemed concerned about me as I grew up. I stuttered severely, but there was no speech therapist at our school. My parents couldn't afford speech therapy, or even knew what it was. We didn't even have transportation to see a speech therapist. We lived in a rural area. Teachers ignored me and didn't seem concerned about my development. We didn't even have a speech course. I never developed many skills except those related to managing a small-dirt farm. I got little training in speaking, reading, or writing. My communication skills made it difficult for me to relate to people. This has haunted me for most of my life. I don't want you to have a similar experience.

If you can't communicate well it will be difficult to relate to people either in school, the workplace, or in your community.

The more you read the more you develop your knowledge. The more you write the greater your facility with language. The more you speak the greater your ability to speak. Speaking, reading, and writing are like muscles: the more you use them the stronger they become.

Be inspired!!!!!!!!!!!

December 30, 2009

19

Lack of Direction

We all at times need some direction. Feel free to come to me or your mother at any such time that you need some directions. At least seek out someone who can help you. Guidance is something I never had much of while growing up. Everything I did was mostly on my own. As soon as I got out of diapers I became my own man.

My mother and father's parents had been farmers who didn't encourage them to get an education. To pursue an education would have meant travel into a city many miles away. This was transportation they couldn't provide. Both my mother and father grew up in isolated-rural areas.

My mother and father couldn't help me much. My mother only finished the eighth grade while my father completed the second grade. They both had to help out on their family's farm. Neither of them knew much about school or the educational culture. It's felt that they were embarrassed about their limited education, and didn't extend a hand to help me. What they did know was mostly old-school-folk knowledge handed down through the generations. They didn't even provide me with any preschool-educational training.

My mother and father were definitely from the old school. They didn't see a need for a Black man to get an education. I think they felt there were only certain kinds of jobs available for a Black man anyway. This idea came from the fact that at one time some Blacks who got an education still had difficulty finding educationally-equivalent jobs.

Why get an education? They never encouraged any of their ten children to get an education beyond high school, and rarely encouraged any of them to graduate high school.

I can never remember my parents once discussing anything about my education. Neither of them ever came to the school to see about my progress. My mother didn't even sign my report card, usually I signed it myself; she was that uninvolved. My father worked out of town.

My older sisters and brothers were lucky to go to school at all, because they had to negotiate a three-mile trail only fit for a wild animal, to travel in order to get to school, or to the bus that would take them to school.

My sisters, brothers, nor relatives were concerned. I was virtually on my own and had to negotiate for myself. Teachers didn't get involved. For a long time we had no counselor, and there was never a social worker.

Had my mother and father known I was planning to attend college they might have tried to discourage me. But they knew nothing of my plans, because they never discussed my plans with me. I simply filled out an application and was accepted. I couldn't get advice from relatives, parents, sisters or brothers, or anyone in the community. They knew very little about colleges. Whatever decision I made was strictly up to me.

I didn't know what to major in, so I ended up taking the path of least resistance. This was partially because I made a failing grade in what I had chosen to major in. I had chosen to major in pre-pharmacy. Even when I graduated I was not sure about what I wanted to do with my life.

I wasn't aware enough to seek help from my high school counselor, college counselor, someone in my community or a nearby community who might have been more knowledgeable. I simply kept going without sufficient direction until it caught up with me.

Don't be like I was. They have counselors in position to help you with the choice of a major or career choice. If you ever get stuck, feel free to seek help from one of your college counselors. If you feel you don't know which way to go, your mother and I are always here to support you.

If you can't see your way out of a situation don't stew in your own stress juices, seek help for your situation. Always make sure you have some clear directions for your life. Don't allow yourself to get bogged down.

Be clear about your directions!!!!!!!!!

January 6, 2010

20

You Can't Be Anything You Want To Be, but You Can Be Better Than What You Are

Politicians and others sometime say, "You can be anything you want to be." I say, "You can't be anything you want to be, but you can be better than what you are."

We all come from a different place. What we're able to become depend on our family background, educational background, social background, motivation, stamina, and intelligence, etc.

Saying that we can be anything we want to be is just a politician's way of encouraging us to make an effort to maximize our potential. It's silly to think that you can start from any place and be anything you want to be. This defies everything logical. Sometime we can start out with too many deficits to overcome the negatives.

If your family didn't give you the kind of background you need, that's a strike against you. If they're poor and live in a poor neighborhood with few resources, this will limit your chances. If your parents can't give you guidance throughout your school years, this will impose another limitation. If they can't afford to help you attend college, this will limit your chances. If they aren't able to give you mental stimulation, confidence, and self-assurance to do well, you're out of luck. What parents pass on to you is definitely a factor in whether you can be all you want to be.

If we're victims of a poor school environment where we received an inadequate education, it will limit our chances of going on to college and improving ourselves. Educational situations are related to family background. An inadequate school situation will increase our chances of being a dropout. It will also decrease the skills that we could have obtained from a better educational situation. A functionally illiterate person cannot be all they could be.

If you live in a situation where there's crime and violence, that's going to be your focus, and will occupy most of your time and energy. If your parents are alcoholics, and there's mental illness in your family, you're going to naturally be preoccupied with these things. If you're worried about where your next meal is coming from, you want have the energy to think about being all you can be. How can a person be anything he wants to be? Someone has told us a lie.

Intelligence is a big factor in us being whatever we want to be. If your intelligence is high enough you might be able to overcome many of the negative situations in your life. If you don't have average intelligence you won't be able to maximize many opportunities.

Obviously, if we're not motivated we aren't going to progress very far. If we aren't motivated we're not going to work hard enough to achieve desirable objectives. But if we're motivated we can overcome many undesirable circumstances. Motivation is a big factor in being what you want to be. You can have the best of circumstances, and if you're unmotivated, you aren't going to maximize your potential. If you're motivated, and came from poor circumstances, you can overcome many negative situations.

Stamina is also an important factor in determining whether you achieve your goals. If you have some physical or mental condition which limits your stamina, you might be unable to carry out your objectives. Such things as asthma, cerebral palsy, being in a wheelchair, having limited sight, etc., can limit us in many ways from reaching our potential. Sometimes motivation can overcome any such factors.

I think what politicians and others meant to say was that if you come from a good home, a decent social environment, go to good schools, have the intelligence, have the motivation, and the stamina; your chances of being whatever you want to be are good—depending upon other resources and opportunities.

Based upon these factors you personally have a good chance of being whatever you want to be. Most of these factors have been favorable in your case. Don't get me wrong, you'll have to work at it. The only problem I noticed you having is your allergies. That shouldn't be too severely limiting. I believe you passed all the other factors with a good grade. Of course, you might feel differently about the situation. Just don't let anybody discourage you or turn you around. You know some people will underestimate your motivation and try to discourage you. It will mainly depend on how motivated you are as to how successful you will become. I have seen people underestimate others motivation on many occasions. I always say, "Do your best and ignore the rest." That, and always try to make a good impression, is the best advice I can give.

Education is a lifetime objective. Rather than get an education for a job, get an education for life. In that way you can't go wrong, because the jobs will come. Think of getting an education as a means of improving yourself. Of course, you want a job after you have improved yourself. Education is for the purpose of making you better than what you are.

When you get this education you should have some skills to go along with this education. An education should teach you to be flexible, creative, and to think for yourself; rather than approach things from a rigid frame of mind. If you involve yourself in your educational process, you can be better than what you are; and can handle any kind of a job in your chosen field.

Remember that once you get your education you will have to understand how to apply it to life and business opportunities. If you can't apply it, much of it has been a waste. I have no doubt you will figure out the game.

Be all you can be!!

January 13, 2010

21

Background

You've probably wondered why I never kept up with your school activities, got involved in the Parent Teacher Organization, or other community organizations; participated in village politics, or ran for any government office. You observed your mother getting involved to some degree. She at least supported you in all of your school activities, and is involved with the church. There are two reasons why I didn't get involved: my background, and the fact that I was tired of dealing with people. But don't you "punk out," the only way to achieve anything is through people.

I observed my parents never getting involved in anything. Until I was in first grade there was no road to my house, only a three-mile trail through the woods. We didn't have any community organizations. All we had was a little rusty, tin-roof, shotgun-shack church. There was no attempt to organize anything that I knew about. My house was a little rusty, tin-roof, shotgun shack that stood at the end of this three-mile trail. We were isolated in our own world for all intent and purpose.

All the people were poor with many children, and lived in the same little type of shotgun shack. They leaked when it rained, and a strong wind could be felt indoors. They were too hot in summer and too cold in winter. I have actually seen mothers send their kids looking for dirt to eat. There was a particular type of clay that some enjoyed as a snack. Some parents would send their kids looking for a type of wild-leafy-green plant that served as a vegetable called "poke salad." They would cook it like you would greens. It had to be cooked a certain way, because they said it could be poisonous.

These people would take their children out of school in September and pick cotton through November. They followed a traditional rural-farm practice. No wonder some of them got behind in school. The boys dropped out of school at an early age, and headed for nearby cities to take jobs. My contact with them was limited.

So I never got indoctrinated into politics or community work. I would be willing to say that it was rare if anyone from our community was allowed, or took the time to attempt voting. I know there was no one involved in politics. We were only concerned with the basics: food, clothing, and shelter. We were happy if we could get these things.

At college I was only concerned with eating, going to class, and doing my assignments. Even in college I didn't socialize much. The stage had already been set. I didn't keep up with local or national affairs—never having been around anyone that was civic minded. The people I was around never discussed civic affairs.

When I came to Chicago, it was a culture shock. I was so happy to have a job that I put all my energy into going to work every day. I didn't meet any civic minded people, and no one encouraged me to get into any organizations. Keep in mind that I was use to being isolated, and didn't have a lot of social skills.

Once when Marcus was in elementary school, I had every intention of joining the PTO, but when I went to the table; the lady at the desk had such a negative attitude. That turned me off for a long time.

I got turned off to people after coming to Chicago. I was always not very social, and I don't know what I expected. But I found the people on the various jobs I obtained reacted to me negatively. Maybe that was just the way people are. I hadn't been around that many people, but I got tired of dealing with their attitudes. They say if you show yourself friendly you will have friends. Maybe I just didn't act friendly.

Don't get me wrong, when you saw me spending a great deal of time at home was because I didn't have gas money to go anyplace. That's why I spent most of my time at home. But I still was a little burnt out on people. I do still like to go places. I would be gone every day if I had gas and transportation. The way I handle my finances, there is nothing for me to do except stay at home. My father stayed in the road, but my mother only went to church and to town. My mother did her best to keep isolated.

I prefer not to join organizations and civic groups. I guess I'm just a basics kind of guy by background. I have a problem because I like to be the HNIC (head nigger in charge), and no one ever wants me to be in charge. At least I don't want to play the games it takes to be in charge. If I can't be in charge I prefer to keep my distance.

I don't want you to be like I was. Make all the friends you can, be a people person, and civic minded.

Be exceptional!!!!!!!!!!

January 20, 2010

22

Career Limitations

I believe I could have gotten further along in my career: possibly majored in pharmacy, engineering, dentistry, law, medicine, or maybe been a tenured teacher with a Ph.D. But my background was such that it would have been almost impossible to major in a more competitive field. I could have done so but it would have taken me a lot longer and a lot more work. All I needed was better social, communication, and academic skills. Of course, I'm not making excuses. What is cannot be changed, and there's no sense crying over spilled milk. There are many factors about my background that placed limits on my potential career.

My mother completed the eighth grade; my father completed the second. All they seem to care about was maintaining that small-dirt farm we lived on. They never encourage me to get an education, but it was something I instinctively wanted to do. Neither of them seemed to care much about their children getting an education—they were from the old school.

First of all, being isolated at the end of a three-mile trail in the middle of nowhere limited me. We didn't get a graded–dirt road to our house until I was in first grade. I was isolated until this time. Being isolated limited my speech development, and hindered my development of social skills. We rarely got a visitor, and even my sisters and brothers rarely talked to me. I had a severe speech impediment.

I didn't start school until I was almost seven-years old. In that school district if your birthday came after September, you had to wait until the next year. When I did start, my speech impediment limited my communications.

I remember in school I was just there. Teachers didn't pay me much attention. As an example, when it came to writing, no teacher took time to show me how to form my letters. A fact that is evident in my writing today. Thank goodness for the computer! No one took a special interest in me. So I drifted along with no one paying me much attention. I did what I was told and obeyed the rules to the best of my ability. Not much was required of me. I attended as often as I could. It was more enjoyable being at school than working around the farm. I don't remember a lot that happened between first and fifth grades.

In fifth grade we had the music teacher for a teacher. She was the only music teacher at the school, and she also taught fifth grade. She spent too much of her time with the music students in practicing for upcoming concerts. Frequently she would leave the classroom and take her students with her to the music room where we listened to her music students practice. Her fifth-grade students were neglected; otherwise, she was a decent teacher. It was a poor district, and it didn't seem they wanted to pay for a fifth-grade teacher and a music teacher, so they had her double up.

In sixth grade I joined the band, and spent too much of my time traveling with the band. I remember I was exempt from several classes every day in order to go to the band room with the band teacher. The band teacher was the sixth-grade teacher also. Again, I guess they didn't want to pay for a band director and a sixth-grade teacher. It was cheaper to combine the functions of the two. The teacher was a poor teacher, and didn't know what he was doing, either as a band director or as a sixth-grade teacher.

In seventh grade I got the same band director as teacher. They bumped him from sixth to seventh grade. One day he asked us to complete an assignment. I picked up a piece of paper from the floor and handed it to him. He put a grade on it and a grade in his grade book. It was the only assignment I remember getting in the sixth and seventh grades. We never had homework. During class time we just sat there and stared out the window. That's enough to retard anyone, especially having my particular background. He refused to teach me how to read music, and was only interested in having me as a body in the marching band, even though I spent a tremendous amount of time in the band room. I had never even had as much as a toy instrument, knew nothing about music, and didn't have the ability to teach myself to read music.

In the eighth grade we had a divided class. There were two sections of the class. The teacher seemed to try harder with the first class than the second. When the second class came to her, I assume she didn't feel like repeating herself. The second class was therefore neglected.

In the ninth and tenth grades there were still two sections of the class. I was always in the section that was thought to have no promise. I always felt that the class I was in got neglected. On top of that I had a severe stuttering habit. We didn't have a speech pathologist in our school district, nor did we have any speech courses. My parents didn't have money, time, or transportation to a town with a speech therapist. I doubt if they even knew what a speech therapist was. We were doing well to have the basics: food, clothing, and shelter.

In the eleventh grade I was suddenly placed in the other section. It was kind of a shock. I had to compete with those students who were considered to have more promise.

After losing two complete years in the sixth and seventh grades, and my other years having been neglected, I suddenly was expected to be able to compete with other students who had had at least some advantage. My teachers throughout my schooling had ignored me for the most part. If I learned anything it was because I did pay strict attention to what was said, not because they paid me any attention.

When I got to college I hadn't developed skills at anything, and didn't know what I wanted to major in. I decided to major in pre-pharmacy; but had severe deficits in chemistry, math, and English. I changed my major from pharmacy to sociology, and it took all my energy just to get through college. I did graduate in three years and a half.

I could have majored in English and been a writer. But my writing and English skills were poor. In addition I hadn't had enough exposure to English to know what writing was about. I found out later that writing could have been one of my strong points. I eventually received two Master's degrees and worked toward a Ph.D. at two different universities.

If you start out with a limited background, you can't be anything you want to be. You'll find that you have too much catching up to do. It'll be difficult to put certain pieces of the puzzle together if you're missing certain information. It'll take too much of your time and energy to pursue certain areas. But if your skills are decent, you can pursue practically anything you want. In other words, you can be anything you want to be if you have the right background, and in addition work hard enough. If your background limits you, you must settle for what you can get.

Be relentless!!!!!!!!!!!

January 27, 2010

23

My Father

Both my parents died before you were born. I've never had a talk with you about them. We've never visited any of my relatives. I'm sure you must have wondered why I never visit any of them, aside from being a long distance away from them. Part of my reasons for coming to Chicago was to put some distance between my relatives and I. It's time that I discuss them with you. When I bring up such topics, it's more to let you know why I am like I am rather than telling you about them. I want you to know why I behave as I do. Most individuals' behavior has antecedents in previous generations. People usually behave much like their parents and significant others, unless they try hard not to. I'll include here only what I feel is relevant to make my point, and will tell you what little I know.

There're a lot of negative things I could tell you about my relatives, but at this point it would serve no purpose. So I won't bring them up. At least, I'm proud to say that none of them ever tried to abuse me sexually. My mother bordered on physically abusing me, but that's something for another day. I will for the most part focus on the positive. I'll discuss my relatives in my next three emails. I hope you can digest the emails.

I've described my parents, siblings, and relatives in other pieces of my writings, but you probably never read any of them. So I'll treat the stories as if you've never heard them before.

First, I'll discuss my father; he's the one I felt closest to. My father was raised in a small town in a rural area of East Texas called Hallsville. He was number eight of sixteen children. His family made their living moving from one sharecropping situation to another. His family didn't own land. He quit school in the second grade because he was needed to work the farm.

After my father married my mother they sharecropped for a while, and then settled down on a small piece of land where we were to live until I left home, and my parents died. The land was family land passed down through my mother's mother. It was a fifty-acre parcel of land.

There was no road to our house, only a trail for three miles off the highway. I don't even see how they managed to haul the lumber to the spot where they built the house. The trail was narrow and had large trenches, with overhanging tree limbs. All the families along this trail were in a similar circumstance. This almost impossible to navigate trail, in anything but a horse or wagon, left us isolated from anything but the most determined traveler.

Soon after I was born my father took a job on the Gulf Coast. He had farmed and worked odd jobs until this time. I was the last of ten children. Jobs were plentiful on the Gulf Coast during and immediately following World War II. It was difficult for my dad to get into the city to a job. He had to first navigate that pig trail, and then catch a ride into the city. There were small cities 20 miles away in either direction. There was nothing but poorly paid farm labor jobs in the rural area where we lived. He came home twice a month, and spent his vacations with us. He spent his vacations fixing up the farm.

My father was getting older as I grew up; he was forty-seven-years old when I was born. When he came home he was always in a rush. Consequently, we never caught a baseball or threw a football to one another. He never even bought me any sports equipment. He wasn't into sports; just concerned about food, clothing, and shelter. We never went to any kind of sporting events together. We actually went few places together, because when I was growing up, we didn't have transportation.

When I was in first grade they constructed a graded red-dirt road through the community. At age eleven I began to drive an old 1951 Fleetline Chevrolet my brother, Wade, had left in a dilapidated-old shed sitting out from the house, that he had built. Wade began teaching me to drive before he left for the Gulf Coast. I would out of necessity, get in the car and go where I wanted to go.

When I started driving I would take my father places, but he would leave me in the car while he went inside to visit. I stuttered severely, after being in an isolated situation all my life. I didn't get an opportunity to socialize or communicate much with other people. My father and siblings would filter any conversation directed at me during my early years. My father leaving me in the car interfered with my communication opportunities.

My father never came to school to see how I was doing, nor did he give me any encouragement toward my education. Since he never got any further than the second grade, he didn't see where an education could benefit his children. This should have had just the opposite effect. We never talked about school. All he ever had to say was to remind me of duties around the farm. I believe his expectations in regard to education were that we would eventually drift away from the educational system. He was never available during school operating hours, being that he worked out of town. He bought me many things that I needed. He bought me coats and shoes when I needed them, and gave me lunch money for school. My father never observed my birthdays, but did buy me Christmas gifts, usually something I needed.

He did take me to visit him on the Gulf Coast for several vacations, beginning when I was six-years old. We never really had much to say to one another. When I visited he usually left me in the care of friends. We never went any place together. But being a young impressionable boy, my father was my role model, and I admired him.

My father retired after twenty years of working in an oil refinery on the Gulf Coast. He came home but never could adapt to life in East Texas. He kept going back and forth between East Texas and the Gulf Coast.

After he retired and returned home, he sometimes put up a front as if he was trying to play his role: he took me fishing and to a few other activities. I took him many places, but I always stayed in the car while he went inside. My father never learned to drive a car.

My brothers said he had other women on the coast that he was spending his money on. I observed him in a friendly manner with one of these women. While we were growing up, I saw him bring this particular woman some of the produce we grew on the farm. One cousin said when my father retired he went by this woman's house and was throwing hundred-dollar bills on the ground, having her children scramble for them.

Once he brought three of these children home with him. I had reason to believe that something was suspicious. These children were awfully close to him. My mother was upset at his boldness. He was basically a good man, simply caught up in time and circumstances. I can never remember him hitting me, or even threatening to hit me.

He finally died in 1988 from some kind of complications with his kidneys. I figured it was because of his heavy drinking in his early days; he was eighty-seven-years old. My father probably rode a bus, but never flew on a plane or rode a train, and never went more than 300 miles from home during his lifetime.

I felt like I never really knew him, but next to my brother, Wade, he was the closest thing to a role model I had.

Be persistent!!!!!!!!!!!

February 3, 2010

24

Mother

My mother was raised in another small East Texas rural town called Harleton. My mother was different from my father. Her parents owned their own land. She worked around the farm with her father until she married my father at twenty-one years of age.

My mother and father settled way back off the beaten path, but she seemed happy being isolated from people. In fact, she seemed upset when they finally constructed the road to our house. While the men were working on the road, she called me in the house and whipped me because I was riding my tricycle near where the men were working. She seemed to feel the road would open up her life to some unwanted consequences. As a young child she would frequently whip me with whatever she could find.

My father did his best to get my mother to move to the Gulf Coast. He made every possible appeal to her, but she refused to move. She was happy on the farm; it was all she ever knew. She was in her domain, with food to eat, rags to wear, and a place to sleep.

All she ever saw for her children was for them to work that dirt farm until they could get away on their own. She seemed to care little about their education. She gave no thought to her children beyond that small farm. She never came to school to see about any of her children. She never tried to prepare or train us for a future.

My mother spent a great deal of her time making sure that her sons labored in the field and did chores, not preparing them for anything beyond the farm. All they could do in the end was managed that small-dirt farm. They had no viable skills.

My brothers said she was harder on the boys than on the girls. She had some strange notion that keeping them busy would keep them out of trouble. She made a vow that she would never be as hard on the girls as her father was on her.

She never put on any fronts: she was cold and hard—not very affectionate, when it came to her children. Maybe I was just the last one and she was burnt out. My mother thought no day was special—everyday was the same—when it came to spending her money. She didn't believe in buying birthday presents, cards, or Christmas gifts.

She never had a job in her life. She fantasized about getting a job, but I felt she had no real intentions in that area. The only jobs she ever had were to manage small farms: from her parent's farm, to sharecropping situations, to her own little farm. Even though the type of little farm she tried to managed was outdated, but she refused to give up until the last child left home.

I started plowing a mule at eleven years of age when the last brother, James, left home. She was strict about the running of the farm, and made me plow that mule from sunup to sunset during growing season. The only thing she allowed to interrupt was rain and the changing of the seasons. I remember her being tight with money where I was concerned. I can never remember any money changing hands between us. This was probably because of her experiences during the Depression.

My mother believed *an idle mind was the devil's workshop*, and believed in keeping me busy. She would be sure there was always some chore to do on the farm. She was obsessed with being sure there were chores to do. Between plowing, herding animals, cutting wood, cutting grass, fixing fences, and whatever else she could find for me to do; she kept me occupied.

One bright spring morning, while waiting for the school bus, she found me on the porch attempting to work some algebra problems. She got so angry that she made me get up early every morning for a while and plow before I went to school. I thought this was unreasonable. But I was determined to continue in school.

We lived on a farm and had all kinds of food: food in all the major food groups, but I can never remember my mother cooking a balanced meal. If she cooked beans, it was just beans and cornbread; if she cooked fried chicken, it was just bread and chicken. Never did she cook meat, bread, and vegetables with some other balanced dish.

I remember when my brother, Wade, wanted to give me his car she was dead-set against it. She knew she didn't have any way to go anyplace, but was against anything that would decrease her isolation, and put her into the modern age. I think if it had been a wagon she would have gladly accepted it.

My mother was born in 1902. She had seen a lot of changes in the world, many of them she was against, or just didn't know how to react to them. In her lifetime there were many inventions: the automobile, TV, the airplane, air conditioning and refrigeration, etc. In fact, most modern inventions occurred or are based on developments during the early part of her life. Yet, things for her never changed. She had been a sharecropper, and wasn't but a few generations out of slavery. She watched all kinds of silly programs on TV, after we finally got one, everything except the news and sports. She wasn't prepared to make all the required adjustments. All she knew that was constant in her life was a plow and a mule, and the general duties on the farm. She didn't travel very much; she never flew on a plane or rode a train or a bus. I can count the times she left home on one hand. She never ventured more than 300 miles away from home, and that was at someone's urging. The only place she went with any consistency was to church. Her ideas were outdated; she was from the old school.

She died in 1989. I didn't feel I really knew her either. She was eighty-eight-years old when she died.

Be understanding!!!!!!!!!!

February 10, 2010

25

Siblings and Relatives

When I became conscious of my environment my third oldest sister was graduating high school, leaving home, and getting married. She was the fourth oldest child. When I started school there were two sisters at home and one brother. My youngest sister was in third grade, and my other sister and brother still at home were juniors in high school. James, my brother, had dropped out for one year, but decided to return. All the others had left home for larger cities. My brother, Wade, had dropped out in the eleventh grade, and headed for the Gulf Coast. I had a problem with my stuttering from being isolated all those years. There was even very little communication between my siblings and I.

My brother, Wade, came back home when I was about in third grade. He got tired of living in the city, and thought things would be better now that we had a road. Everyone resented the trail situation, though no one spoke of it, and it was in the late 1950s. He took me to Cub Scott meetings, ball games, county fairs, school activities and other places. He would keep my hair cut and give me money.

Wade never had much to say, but he was a great help to me. At age eleven he began teaching me how to drive. It was a sad moment when he left again. But when I turned sixteen he gave me his 1959 Chevrolet Impala, and for years he kept in touch—buying me parts for the car and giving me money. I would frequently visit him on the Gulf Coast.

The other nine siblings I didn't have much of a relationship with. When I was younger my sister, Lethamae, would buy me some clothes on occasions. Some of them visited frequently and some visited infrequently. They were all away and we didn't get much of an opportunity to bond.

I do remember that none of them came to my high school graduation, gave me a gift, or congratulations. Wade came through for my eight-grade graduation, but I didn't hear from him during high school graduation. Only one nephew came to my wedding, of all nine brothers and sisters. None of them came to my college graduation either. With the exception of Wade and Lethamae, none of the rest ever gave me a birthday card or even an occasional Christmas gift.

My oldest brother, Luther, came to see me once in college. He was the only one who came to see me in college. None of the rest even attempted to make any contact. No one else visited or even wrote me a letter. I didn't even hear from my parents.

My siblings weren't negative or positive, but rather neutral and uninvolved. Most of them didn't give me money because it was a scarce commodity.

My siblings never had decent jobs. Wade did construction work, and Luther drove a truck. Those were the best jobs any of them ever had. One reason was because they grew up on the farm, and never learned how to do anything except plow and hoe. None of them had any additional training. I was the only one to attempt college—out of ten children. They, out of necessity, were only concerned with the basics: food, clothing, and shelter. If they could get these things they were happy. They learned this back on the farm.

Three of my brothers and one sister have passed on to glory. I still have four sisters and a brother alive. Wade, I hadn't heard from in many years. I really don't know if he is dead or alive.

I only met one grandparent: my father's mother. She always asked my father questions about me, but never talked directly to me. When I was a young boy she was in her nineties. I saw her as cold and lacking in affection. She lived close by, but I rarely saw her. I can never remember her coming to our house.

I knew two of my father's brothers. One lived in Arizona, and came to visit every Christmas, but he never brought me a gift. One other brother lived in a town nearby. We would visit him, but I wouldn't go inside. I met several of my father's sisters, but had no close relationship with any of them. They were too preoccupied with their own families.

My mother had brothers who live in towns nearby, but most of them never visited us. Several of them did visit, but we maintained no close contact. My mother also had several sisters who maintained little contact.

I had many relatives, but had a relationship with few of them. Most of them didn't visit us on the farm. Relatives seemed very distant. Relatives were insignificant in my life. I didn't even know who many of my cousins were. I came to find out later who was a cousin. I did associate with several cousins, some I considered close friends. I figured most of my relatives didn't visit because of the inconvenience of coming to a place that didn't have indoor plumbing. We rarely had visitors.

These people and circumstances made me who and what I am, whether that's good or bad.

I could tell you more about my family, but due to time and space limitations, I will stick with "just the facts."

Be consistent!!!!!!!!!!!!

February 17, 2010

26

My Community

I've written a lot in past emails about where I grew up. I can't talk about this place enough in my own mind. The reason I keep mentioning it is because it made me what I am today—whether good or bad.

We lacked so many necessities. Here I want to talk about the negatives in my community and the surrounding area. There was an atmosphere of racism, prejudice, bigotry, and discrimination. There were few jobs. Blacks didn't vote: hence all elected officials were white. Blacks had difficulty getting necessary services provided. There were few Black-male role models. There was hardly any integration.

What I mean by racism, prejudice, discrimination and bigotry is that for example, it took the county from 1929 to 1954 to build a simple-dirt road from the main highway. We only had a three-mile trail to our front door. You can imagine how difficult travel was for us not having a road. We could only travel by horse or horse and wagon. Part of the reason we didn't have that road was because of being disfranchised.

Restaurants, libraries, sporting events, motels and hotels, bathroom facilities, and water fountains were all segregated. Some Blacks did have a road, even though it was a dirt road. Many of them didn't even have that dirt road. The old idea that Blacks new their place and stayed in it was alive and well.

There are four things that all children need: a well-functioning family, a good school, a good spiritual background, and institutions that will promote the growth and development of the individual and family. If any one of these things is missing from a child's life it'll be difficult to lead a healthy life.

Those who continue to survive and function without a healthy exposure to any of these institutions are indeed lucky. They should thank the Balance in the Universe. They don't need Christmas presents during the season, because they already have the greatest gift in the world—life itself. I am one of those who don't worry about Christmas gifts, for I am truly blessed—and I know it.

I attended a backward—rural school in East Texas during the 1950s and 1960s. We were one step beyond the one-room schoolhouse commonly depicted in the literature throughout the early part of our history in this country. Some of the books we used were hand-me-downs from the white school, and had several names in them that obviously weren't passed down from upper–level classes. Even some of the desk we inherited had names carved in them that I was unfamiliar with. I had a stuttering habit, and no one paid much attention to me. Expectations for me were low. In my perception teachers didn't try hard because of their low expectations for most students.

I never heard any of the teachers or students talk about anything but basic living from day to day. There were no discussions of local, state, or national politics. When the Civil Rights Movement took place there were very few discussions of it. We never even discussed Black history.

I wasn't encouraged to attend college, trade school, and certainly no one tried to help me get a scholarship or a loan for college. It seemed as far as they were concerned it was good riddance, and I should feel lucky to graduate high school.

I frequented a small community church. It was on a dusty-dirt road in the middle of nowhere. Most community people weren't motivated to become members. It had a potbellied stove for winter heating, and was without fan or air conditioning in summer. The pews were of rough-hewn pine, with splinters that would grab and tear your clothing in a hot second, and nothing was ever dusted.

We didn't have a regular minister; most of what we got was lay instruction. Only six or seven people attended each Sunday. There was no Sunday school, Bible class, or youth programs. We didn't have programs during the major holidays like most churches. There were no training programs for the youth; since, I was the only young person attending.

My family was also dysfunctional. My mother and father had a sharecropper's mentality, they believed in doing things the old way. My mother saw to it that I spent most of my spare time plowing a mule until it was time to leave the farm. Neither my mother nor father encouraged me to get an education. My father was out of the home for a large portion of the time, and couldn't serve as a decent role model.

All of us who lived in the area and survived were lucky. There were no institutions to aid in the growth and development of the family or the individual, other than the inadequate ones mentioned. There were no organized sports, playgrounds, or community centers.

I was blessed more than most coming from my community. Most of the males dropped out of school and gravitated to larger cities, taking whatever jobs they could find. The girls usually graduated from high school, but still had to take whatever jobs they could find. I was fortunate to get three degrees, and to work on a Ph.D. in sociology at two different Midwestern universities. I held adequate social work jobs for fifteen years. I am currently on disability, but consider myself lucky to just be alive.

This is the environment from which I come. It's mind boggling to think about what I could have accomplished had all the major institutions been in place and fully functioning.

I had greater ambitions than I was able to realize; but if I was able to advance this far with my background, I know you can build a successful career.

Be blessed!!!!!!!!!!!!

February 24, 2010

27

How Slavery Affected the Black Family

It's believed that the history of African Americans causes them to be the way they are today: they continue to be affected by pre-slavery, slavery, post-slavery, and modern-day society. Slavery has had the greatest affect. Many will argue that this is not the case. They will question, how could this be? Slavery ended approximately one-hundred-fifty years ago. They should have gotten over slavery by now. Besides the Black family was in better condition many years ago than it is today. Anyone who knows anything about the conditioning process will agree that slavery has had a lasting affect.

I assure you that such things as family abuse, out of wedlock children, single-parent families, lack of communication in the family, unwillingness of males to remain with the family, domestic abuse and violence in the family, and lack of unity in the family; are all related to the years prior to slavery, slavery, and the years after slavery.

Other groups appeared on the African shores over 10,000 years ago. We allowed them to become a part of our social, political, religious, educational, and marital institutions. As their numbers grew they began to take control of these institutions. Once inside they began to dismantle these institutions. They suggested that African institutions were inferior, and theirs were superior. We then got confused over our own norms and values. Some of these groups began to marry into native tribes. When the offspring were born they usually took the side of their fathers in any tribal disputes—frequently to the detriment of the tribe.

In many cases when war broke out we disbanded and headed for the hills and jungles, creating more tribes and disorganized societies. We continued this way until the slave trade. When the slave trade came along we were too confused, chaotic and disorganized to fight against it. We fought but could not fight against their weapons. In addition, we were so confused, that some chiefs use the situation as a money making opportunity. The chiefs helped to capture the natives for the slave trade.

During the Middle Passage we were divided according to tribe, culture, and language, before being placed on the ships for other parts of the world. We were divided so we could not relate to one another, and could not come together in unity for the purpose of rebelling. We were treated like animals, and degraded in every possible way, and saw each other abused so much that we lost respect for one another. Africans were conditioned to feel impotent, to lack self-esteem, to lack self-worth, and to have a poor self-image.

In slavery we were again treated as animals, sold as property, used as studs and concubines, and sent from one plantation to another. Slaves could not be responsible for their families when they were allowed to form them. In many cases they were used for breeding purposes.

When we first stepped off the boat and were sold to various plantations, it was on the basis of language, culture, and tribe. On the plantation, we were not allowed to travel from one plantation to another without a pass. Again, this was so we would not rebel.

The slave master pimped the slaves, and we began to imitate his behavior with our own women. We lost touch with our children, and had only impersonal relationships with them. We learned to treat our women as sex objects: using them only for sex. The slave master in most cases maintained priority with our women.

After slavery we maintained similar relationships as had existed in slavery. Though marriage was legal, we still carried over many of our difficulties. We had difficulty caring for our families. We couldn't get an adequate education, find decent employment, get decent housing, or maintain relationships with our families.

Some say slavery didn't cause any of our current problems, but I beg to disagree. Even it they were better some years ago, such conditions are bound to have an exponential effect. They multiply in effect as time goes along.

Today, we are still trying to pimp our women. We run from family relationships, have difficulty with communication and unity, as well as unable to relate to our children. The process began many years ago, and has been maintained throughout history. It was most apparent in slavery, but has been just as effective since slavery.

Forgive me if I tend to occasionally repeat something from one week to the next. It's hard to keep track of what I have said in previous emails.

Be creative!

March 3, 2010

28

Stolen Legacy

George G. M. James wrote a book called *Stolen Legacy*. It would be good to compare in your own mind what he says about traditional Greek philosophy, with what Europeans say about this philosophy. Sometimes in your college career you will read about the origins of this so-called Greek philosophy. Most likely you will read about the origins of this philosophy in a history course called Western Civilization.

James says that traditional Greek philosophy is really stolen Egyptian philosophy. Greek philosophers were given credit for this philosophy, and it's the basis of Western philosophy. The Greeks were not the authors of the philosophies they are credited with; it was Egyptians that were the originators, and Egypt is in North Africa.

After nearly five-thousand years of prohibition against the Greeks, they were finally permitted to enter Egypt for the purposes of their education. In James's book he says that the immigration of Greeks to Egypt for the purpose of their education, began as a result of the Persian invasion (525 B.C.), and continued until the Greeks gained possession of that land and access to the Royal Library, through the conquests of Alexander the Great.

When Alexander the Great invaded Egypt, one of the first things that he and his companions and armies would do, would be to search for the treasures of the land and capture them. These were kept in temples and libraries and consisted of gold and silver out of which the gods and ceremonial vessels were made, and sacred books and manuscripts kept both in libraries and in the "Holy of Holies" of Temples.

James suggests that this indeed was the great opportunity which Alexander gave Aristotle and enabled him and his pupils to plunder, pillage, and carry off as many books as they wanted from the Royal Library and to convert it into a research centre. When Alexander invaded Egypt he looted and burned the libraries and temples, and took what books he wanted for himself. He made a library of his own, and distributed the rest to then Greek philosophers. The Greek philosophers plagiarized these books. The amount of books ascribed to Aristotle was a physical impossibility for any single man in a lifetime. Aristotle was supposed to have spent twenty years under Plato from whom he could learn nothing. Plato couldn't have instructed Aristotle in the many various subjects contained in these books because he had no such knowledge. Plato was not knowledgeable to teach Aristotle. The books credited to Aristotle were probably in circulation before Aristotle's time, and he couldn't have produced them or introduced the new ideas in them.

This was the ancient custom and certainly one of the ways in which the Greeks received their education from Egyptians. Alexandria was converted into a Greek city, a centre of research and the capital of the newly created Greek empire, under the rule of Ptolemies. Egyptian culture survived and flourished, under the name and control of the Greeks, until the edicts of Theodosius in the 4th century A.D., and that of Justinian in the 6th century A.D., which closed the Mystery Temples and schools.

From the sixth century B.C. therefore to the death of Aristotle (322 B.C.) the Greeks made the best of their chance to learn all they could about Egyptian culture; most students received instructions directly from the Egyptian priest.

For example the maxim "know thyself," was attributed to Socrates, when the Egyptians Temples carried this inscription on the outside addressed to those who entered, long before Socrates.

Aristotle died in 322 B.C not many years after he had been aided by Alexander the Great to secure the largest quantity of scientific books from the Royal Libraries and Temples of Egypt.

James felt that most of the gods came into Greece from Egypt. Herodotus, a Greek of the 5th century, wrote approximately 2,500 years ago that early Greeks received their knowledge, wisdom, and understanding from Egypt. James refutes the Euro-centric myth that the origin of Western philosophy is Greek. It has been taught in every educational facility and university that the Greeks originated Western philosophy.

Such teachings remained for generations and centuries in the form of tradition in Egypt, until the conquest of Egypt by Alexander the Great, and the movement of Aristotle and his school to compile Egyptian teaching and claim it as Greek philosophy. After the conquest of Egypt by Alexander the Great, and the seizure and looting of the Royal Library at Alexandria, Aristotle's plan to usurp Egyptian philosophy was subsequently carried out by members of his school.

It's indeed surprising how, for centuries, the Greeks have been praised by the Western World for intellectual accomplishments which belong without a doubt to the Egyptians or the people of North Africa. This philosophical contribution to civilization was made by the Egyptians and the African continent, but not by the Greeks. The Egyptians even taught Pythagoras and the Greeks what mathematics they knew. Not only did the Egyptians give us the philosophies but also the arts and sciences.

There are those who will say that Africa hasn't made any major contributions to the world. Had the Greeks not stolen African philosophy, Africans might have enjoyed a status of respect among the nations of the world. Instead the historical world opinion is that the African continent is backward, that its people are backward, and that their civilization is also backward.

Be knowledgeable!!!!!!!!!!!!!!!

March 10, 2010

29

The New Jinx

When I was growing up, to be jinxed was to be the victim of someone who had cast a negative spell. The one who was considered to be causing the jinx was a type of sorcerer, someone to be looked down upon. My older brothers would use the term all the time by saying, "You jinxed me, or I've been jinxed." This meant they had been affected in a way to cause the negative outcome of one of their life events. The term was used in connection with the concept of voodoo. But anyone could jinx another person just by being present. It was the one nebulous catchall category under which you could blame all your problems.

Usually when someone was trying to accomplish something in particular, and failed, they would say they were jinxed. I have heard this term applied when an individual failed to accomplish many different things. It spoke negatively about the person being accused, for he was being accused of a type of witchcraft.

Today, racial discrimination can be seen as the new jinx, because it's that vague thing that's the cause of Black people's problems. We attribute many of our problems to racial discrimination, when some of our problems are due to some internal issues within the Black community. For example when the character J. J. on the sitcom "Good Times" was questioned about some problems he was having—he said, "Remember, I'm the victim of 400 years of discrimination and oppression." This statement is true without a doubt. Some people use such statements to justify their misgivings in a racist society. The truth is racism does cause many problems in the Black community.

Of course, some wonder what history has to do with most of our present-day problems. It shouldn't be too hard for us, especially the erudite, to see how history is usually passed on from generation to generation. It's almost as if there was a genetic factor responsible for passing on our history, because we repeat many historical patterns.

Our history causes us many problems, but this history has affected us in so many ways that it confounds us even today. Take for example the idea that Blacks were used as studs in slavery; and sent from plantation to plantation to mate with other slaves. Used for breeding purposes and hard work on the plantation. Not given any sense of responsibility as a husband or father, and simply seen as chattel. Young Black men lacked role models. It's believed that this is the basis of the fact that many Black males are still going from female to female, not taking any sense of responsibility for the children they bring into the world.

The Black male observed the slave master as he was a type of pimp over the Black male and female. The Black male has closely observed this role very carefully over the generations. Subsequently, some Black males have seen the role of the pimp in modern society as the most revered role in the Black community. We're still trying to be pimps and procurers of our women. Men were seen by the women as irresponsible and objects of sex only—not as protectors and providers. The female learned that she could not depend on the Black male.

Whereas racism doesn't cause all our problems, it's the likely progenitor of many of them. Even though such historical events occurred many years ago, they somehow got passed on with each new generation. Today we have a situation where such problems have gotten out of control.

Take violence for example: we learned to hate ourselves and our characteristics. This soon turned into self-hate. In this case we turned all our negativity toward each other. When you have self-hate you'll most likely dislike those who look like you, and are the closest to you. Blacks kill each other also because they're the most readily available targets. Those responsible don't always make readily available targets.

It's sometimes hard to see how the problems began many years ago, and continues today. Some of our young and old leaders have historical amnesia. The original problem is so far removed from them that they can't see how historical problems affect us today. So they go along with the majority in saying such conditions as pre-slavery, slavery, and post-slavery has absolutely no affect on the behavior of Blacks today. But such conditions are the genesis of our experience in the Western world and cause us to behave as we do.

We have blamed our historical jinx on racism, but we will be unable to go on throughout our present and future days to attribute our problems to racism. At some point we'll have to say, "We have met the enemy and it is us."

Racism is still to us our modern-day jinx, because it's that one broad negative condition under which we can lump all of our problems.

Be historically correct!!!!!!!!!!

March 17, 2010

30

Things That Will Haunt You for a Long Time

Be careful how you live your life. It's possible to have certain persistent thoughts haunt you for a long time. These thoughts aren't necessarily deleterious, just persistent. If you want to prevent these types of thoughts from haunting you, don't allow the notions to become part of your reality.

Nip these situations in the bud before allowing them to manifest themselves. If you do you won't have to worry about seeing such events in your dreams. Such thoughts will sometimes intrude into your dream life, and become a persistent factor in your memory.

Remember, it's not the event itself that has an affect on your life, but how you perceive the event. Some of your life experiences will naturally stay with you much longer than others. But it depends on how you handle the event as to how long it continues to affect you.

The following are a list of things that could haunt you for a long time if you don't handle them right:

(1). A sexy girl that wanted to give you an opportunity, but you decided not to take it.

(2). Situations where you responded more negatively to others than what was called for, and you regretted it.

(3). A promise a parent made but did not follow through.

(4). A teacher whom you felt did not treat you fairly.

(5). Being punished for something you didn't do.

(6). A close friend who betrayed you.

(7). A girl who didn't like you no matter how hard you tried to please her.

(8). A relative who was mean and nasty. Other people won't affect you as much as the attitudes of relatives. You come to expect a nasty attitude from others in your environment.

(9). A girl that had the perfect body, the most beautiful face, and the most wonderful personality.

(10). Relationships that you couldn't make right no matter how hard you tried.

(11). Memories of the Christmas and birthday you got the perfect gifts.

(12). Memories of the Christmas and birthday you didn't get the gifts you wanted.

(13). Images in your mind of the nice girl that got away, when you liked her, and knew she liked you.

(14). Things that you should or should not have said.

(15). How you shouldn't have let someone put you down.

(16). A dream that you showed up for class, but it was a holiday.

(17). A dream that you failed a test.

(18). How you shouldn't have behaved in that particular way in that situation.

(19). How you made a wrong choice.

(20). How you went to the wrong school.

(21). How you pursued the wrong girl after having several choices.

(22). How you should have studied harder for a particular test.

(23). How you should have spoken up about something important, but didn't say anything.

(24). Thoughts that you should have done some aspect of your life differently.

(25). A failing grade will stay on your mind for a long time.

(26). Thoughts of letting a smart mouth outwit you, when you could have spoken up for yourself.

(27). Thoughts of letting a bully pick on you, or someone else push you around.

(28). Dreams that you are late for a class, late for a test, or was locked out of a class after being more than a few minutes late.

(30). Dreams that you showed up for a test, but the test was over, and the professor and the students had left.

These are just a few of the possible thoughts that could linger in your mind. Such thoughts will sometimes affect you for a long time. Naturally, some of these persistent thoughts will not be true for you, and you might have certain others. Depending on the individual, such persistent thoughts will change over time, due to the nature of your experiences. It also depends on the nature of the experiences as to how persistent they are in your thoughts and dreams. Don't allow such thoughts to cripple you.

Be invigorated!!!!!!!!!

March 24, 2010

31

Why I Don't Visit My Relatives

You never asked me any questions about it, but you must wonder why I don't visit any of my relatives. Even though we're a long distance from any of them, I could visit more frequently than I do. I know it's more to why you don't ask than simply the fact that we don't communicate that much anyway. I visited my mother and father on a regular basis until my father died in 1988 and my mother died in 1989. I had some negative feelings about even them, but figured I owed them that much respect. I take the Bible seriously when it says to *honor thy mother and father*. After all, they did bring me into thc world and cared for me until I could care for myself. Before you were born I made several attempts to visit some of my brothers and sisters, but figured by their behavior that they didn't want to be bothered.

My sisters and brothers all live not more than three-hundred miles away from where we grew up. Few of them ever visited us in the country on a frequent basis. One sister came to see us rarely; another sister came when she had a problem; one sister did visit for her summer vacations; another sister visited infrequently; and another sister who lived no more than twenty miles away, came almost every weekend. Of course, I think some of them saw a trip of a few miles as a trip around the world.

I had a brother who came almost every year at Christmas; another brother who rarely came to visit; and one brother who lived a few miles away who visited on frequent occasions.

Even other relatives rarely visited. I would spend months without seeing a visitor. I spent most of my childhood in isolation. I didn't know if it was my parent's ability to sustain relationships, or if it was the fact that we lived so far off the beaten path. Of course, we didn't have a navigable road to our house until I was in first grade. We had no indoor plumbing or telephone. I figured most folks didn't want to be bothered with this situation. Don't get me wrong, occasionally other relatives would visit, but again these visits were rare.

Another reason why I don't visit them is because most of my sisters and brothers never showed me any consideration. Only one brother and one sister ever bought me a Christmas present: one brother was always there for me, and a sister bought me a few Christmas gifts when I was a young boy. None of them ever recognized my birthday with a card. I never had a birthday party during my first twenty-one years of life. Neither my mother or father ever gave me a birthday present or birthday card; no one ever sang happy birthday to me, cooked me a cake, and my mother was good at cooking cakes. Come to think of it, they didn't even recognize your birthday at school.

A sister who lived nearby was kind enough to take me to my eighth-grade graduation, and my brother bought me a gift, but when I graduated high school, none of them came to my graduation or gave me a graduation present. They didn't even say congratulations. It was the same for my graduation from college and my wedding. One sister did give me a gift for my wedding a few years after I was married. One brother stuck by me for a while. He supported me through high school: gave me money and bought me a car. He offered me absolutely no support in college.

In college I had one sister to send me twenty-five dollars near my graduation. None of the rest wrote me a letter, sent money, or a care package. One brother did come by to visit because his mother-in-law lived in that small college town.

I tried to be amenable to all of them, by visiting after I graduated college, but finally figured out that if they didn't care enough to visit me when I was growing up, why should I visit them now? Since they have responded this way, I'm positive they don't want to be bothered with me. This is why I don't have a close relationship with any of my relatives. Why travel all that distance to see someone who doesn't want to be bothered. That's just my perception. I know my perceptions can be faulty at times.

Be supportive!!!!!!!!

March 31, 2010

32

Bad Blood

I don't like to bring up the negative, but from second or third grade I can remember having a feeling there was bad blood in my family. Especially since my immediate family had a few cases of schizophrenia. There was no history of schizophrenia but apparently my mother and father's recessive gene combination, and the social conditions they lived in, produced some schizophrenia in some of their children. When I was in third grade this schizophrenia began to manifest itself in some family members, the talk of voodoo became prevalent, and other conversations about bad blood were spoken.

The recessive gene combination along with the conditions under which we lived was generative of the condition of schizophrenia. I listened to my mother, father, sisters, and brothers blame every condition in the family on bad blood. My eyes would get red in the spring, and they would blame this on bad blood. I think eye allergies are quite common in this country, not necessarily related to bad blood, but they didn't understand the nature of allergies. Any medical condition that developed they would attribute to bad blood.

This notion of bad blood was common in other families. Some families talked about bad blood of members who ended up in prison. Others talked about bad blood for those who just generally did stupid things. But children who heard this spoken of about their family generally had some negative feelings associated with it, to the extent that it influenced what they became.

I heard my relatives talk in general about bad blood to the extent that I internalized this idea about our bloodline. When there was nothing wrong with our bloodline. I internalized this idea to such an extent that I developed an inferiority complex. I also had many frustrations and internal conflicts. There was also some talk in the family about having been affected by some type of voodoo which had affected the family's bloodline. What a ridiculous notion for a young boy to have about his family. Such a notion could be very destructive for one's future. When considering the fact that I stuttered, was under-socialized, and isolated; all this contributed to my inferiority complex.

I had such a belief in my family as having a bad bloodline that it colored everything I did: I was always nervous, full of anxiety, and unsure of myself. One day the science teacher was trying to get some students to go to a nearby city to give a badly needed blood donation. He approached me privately and asked if I wanted to give blood, "I have bad blood I said." I had actually internalized, in my own way, that there was something wrong with my family's blood. And I had gathered all this from my family's discussions. After that the science teacher stated in class without referring to me in particular, "There is no such thing as bad blood, unless you have some type of blood disease. Some people even feel there blood is bad because they have been affected by voodoo." He went on to say that, "Even with voodoo, unless someone put something deleterious in your food, there was little chance of it affecting you." The science teacher must have been familiar with folk notions of bad blood and voodoo. I considered that he was simply taking the statement I made about having bad blood and refuting it.

Somehow as I grew up I did feel inferior and ashamed of my bloodline; mainly because some folks in my family believed in voodoo and because of the schizophrenia in our family. You should never feel ashamed of your family, whether on Frances's or my side of the family. Such a thing can cause you to have an inferiority complex for the rest of your life.

Unconsciously, I believe I lived in dread that people would find out about my background, as if I was an imposter trying to pull the wool over everyone's eyes. But there is no need to live your life that way, live your life as an open book. In that way you won't be hiding and darting behind shadows. In other words, you have nothing to hide. You are for real and always have been.

The only way to have bad blood is to have a blood disease. If you don't have this you can rest assured there is noting wrong with your family's bloodline.

Every individual is different and has a unique contribution to make to society. God has made you with your own potential and capabilities. Don't worry about where you came from, just think about where you're going.

Remember, for schizophrenia to manifest itself in a family or individual requires a poor social and psychological environment as well as an unfavorable recessive gene combination.

Be level headed!!!!!!

April 7, 2010

33

Hair Time

Do you remember when you asked Frances to have her hairdresser texturize your hair? When you had it done it was a little too straight, and you looked like a Black person with some heavy European ancestry. I don't think you liked it quite that straight. I don't know what it is with our hair, but we're constantly, it seems, trying to imitate other groups' way of wearing their hair. Although, I'm sure that was not your conscious intent.

This battle with our hair is a long story, one that I cannot adequately address in just a few lines. However, I want to try and elaborate on the nature of this situation. I think most Blacks go through such a phase with their hair. I wanted to say something then, but decided to let you do what you wanted. There're reasons why we wish to imitate other groups in this fashion, and we need to examine why we constantly have problems with our hair. If we're not imitating other groups to make our hair straighter or curlier, we simply cut it all off. It seems that we would rather do anything than wear our hair the way it naturally grows. We see it as to kinky or nappy.

Even for the most conscious of Black people, many of them don't feel comfortable unless they straighten, curl, or relax their hair. Some of the staunch advocates for civil and human rights wear a texturizer in their hair. It has gotten to the point where it seems natural to pervert the way our hair naturally grows.

There's a history to the attitude we have toward our hair. Of course, not only do we have an attitude about our hair, but we seem not to like our eyes, noses, lips, feet, buttocks, etc. But I only want to consider hair in this email. The other qualities are for another email at another time and date.

It's my conception that we began to feel inferior about our hair and other qualities when we first made contact with other groups over 10,000 years ago. Somehow when we came in contact with these other groups we felt our hair was inferior. Since Blacks are the only ethnic group to have the quality of hair that they have.

We felt inferior about our hair and began to try and imitate other groups in the way they wore their hair. We felt that other groups had more to offer us than we had to offer ourselves. We began to imitate these other groups in many ways—especially the way they wore their hair. We associated superiority with these groups from the time they appeared on the African shores.

Out of our inferiority, we developed self-hate which led us to dislike the quality of our hair. This self-hate caused us to dislike most things about ourselves. At this point we referred to kinky or nappy hair as bad and straight hair as good. If we are pressed we'll say straight hair is easy to manage hair.

Our problem is that with as many hairdressers as there are in the Black community, they could come up with products and instruments that are designed to take care of Black peoples' hair. We can't simply say our hair is not easy to manage, and go on imitating other groups in their hairstyles. If we had equipment not designed for other groups' hair, our hair would be easier to manage. But we go on day after day frying, teasing, and squeezing our hair.

We use so many different chemicals in our hair, and frequent the hair dressers so often, that some women become prematurely bald. The chemicals are often too harsh for our hair. But we would do almost anything to keep our hair straight, what we call more presentable.

Most other groups simply wash and set their hair, rather than spend long hours at the hairdresser. Only those other groups with a great deal of money frequent the hairdresser, while Blacks across the board spend an exorbitant amount of cash to keep their hair permed and straight. Some of this money could be better spent on other things in the household. Mothers who once did their daughters' hair with a hot comb, now start them at an early age going to the beauty shop. No wonder by the time they're fifty their hair is burnt out, and their hair starts falling out.

When they turn bald they get a straight-hair wig. We need a better way of taking care of our hair. It's time to wear our hair the way it naturally grows, and to have more respect for what God made. We go to church Sunday after Sunday and listen to the minister talk about God and how He loves us all, and is no respecter of persons, but he has some type of texturizer in his hair.

If he truly feels that God loves us all the way we're fearfully and wonderfully made, why does he need to pervert the nature of his hair. Just because our hair is not like other groups it doesn't mean there's anything wrong with it—it's just different. There is a reason for the variety God made in the universe, so man would have an infinite variety of choices for his pleasure. I'm sure he never meant for us all to run around imitating each other.

Be serious!

April 14, 2010

34

Some Things to Think About

I don't know many of these kinds of stories. In addition, I don't think I'm very good at storytelling; mainly because none of my parents, sisters, brothers, or relatives told me any stories as I was growing up. We never even had much storytelling in my early years of school. One man who was visiting a neighbor introduced storytelling to me. But he didn't stay in the neighborhood long. We were weak on communication, as I have said many times. We were in poverty in more than one way. Storytelling is usually a big tradition in the Black family. That's another reason why I encourage you to take as much speech as you can, so you will never have any handicaps with respect to communicating.

Pretty Swan/ Ugly Duck

Once a farmer placed an egg under a mother duck who was preparing to hatch her other eggs. He mistakenly placed a swan's egg under the duck with the other duck eggs. He had both swans and ducks on his farm. When the eggs hatched and the mother duck took her ducklings to the pond, the swan looked at the other ducks and looked at his reflection in the water. He had a long neck and thought he was ugly compared to the other ducks. Finally, he came back to the pond and met a swan. He figured out that he was actually a swan rather than a duck, and wasn't an ugly duck after all, but a pretty swan.

It's important to realize that sometimes an ugly duck can be a pretty Swan. It's important to realize who you really are.

The Elephant and the Stake

When an elephant in a circus is a young elephant the owner chains it to a heavy stake to keep it from getting away. The elephant is conditioned to this stake after trying all his might to set himself free, but he can't. When the elephant is fully grown it's chained to a much smaller stake, and it won't try to break free, because it has been conditioned to the larger stake. With this smaller stake the elephant could get away if he only tried to break free, but he won't because of his conditioning.

Conditioning is a very powerful tool, and is applicable to many situations. Don't let past conditioning control the rest of your life. You may have outgrown past conditioning, but still allow it to control your life.

The Scorpion and the Duck

Once there was a scorpion who wanted to get across a river. Of course, scorpions can't swim. The scorpion saw a duck about to cross the river, so he asked the duck to let him ride on his back. The duck being of a kind and gentle nature agreed to let the scorpion ride on his back across the river. Everything was going fine until they got about midway the river, and for no particular reason the scorpion stung the duck. The scorpion's venom is poisonous to other smaller animals.

Before going down the duck asked the scorpion, "Why did you sting me, didn't you know we were both going to sink and die?"

The Scorpion replied, "That's my nature, it's what I do."

Certain things have certain natures, and no matter how you try to appeal this nature it or they will react the same old way.

The Rattlesnake

A woman was driving down the highway and saw a diamondback rattlesnake on the side of the road. It was pretty in its array of earth-tone colors; it was cold. She picked it up and brought it home. She placed it by the fire and let it warm up, and gave it something to eat. The rattlesnake hissed and struck her in her neck.

The woman asked, "Why did you do that, after I brought you in out of the cold, warmed you up and fed you."

The snake replied, "You knew I was a snake when you took me in."

No matter how you treat some people or animals they will still respond like that snake, because it is in their nature.

Let's Pretend

Once Tony went to a party hosted by Larry his cousin. He met Gail at the party. He had known Gail for several years. He had gone to the same school with her for several years. They were what you could call friends. The party was in full swing. All the young men were attempting to demonstrate their prowess by getting their girlfriends in a corner and attempting to make love to them. Neither Tony nor Gail came with anyone. Tony was embarrassed because he didn't have a date to be with. Gail and Tony were the only ones at the party without a partner.

He told Gail, "Lets get on the bed and pretend, we don't have to make love for real. I'm just so embarrassed with everyone else making out."

Gail replied, "OK, I guess it would be OK to pretend."

Tony and Gail started kissing, and Tony got carried away. He started touching her all over her body.

Gail said, "Wait a minute, I thought we were just pretending."

Tony said, "I'm just trying to make it look real."

Before long Tony was pushing aside her panties and sliding his penis in her vagina.

"Stop she said, you're going in."

Tony replied, "How about that."

Be careful what you let people talk you into; what you believe is pretend could be real and serious to them.

Don't be an Idiot

Once, Sammy visited his girlfriend, Susan. Susan's parents weren't home, and Sammy talked her into going into the bedroom. They got in the bed and began hugging and kissing. The situation progressed to touching her all over her body. Finally, he pushed her panties aside and placed his fingers in her vagina.

Sammy, being inexperienced asked, "Can I have some sex baby."

To which Susan replied, "No!"

Realize when you are ahead in the game, and don't ask stupid-idiotic questions.

Shake Your Head

My high school principal told a story once about World War II while fighting the Japanese. They were deep in the jungle. He got in a hand-to-hand combat situation. Suddenly a Japanese soldier jumped at him from out of the underbrush. He swung his machete and cut the Japanese head off.

The Japanese soldier said, "You missed."

The blade was so sharp his head didn't move.

To which he replied, "Shake your head."

The Japanese soldier shook his head, and indeed his head fell off.

Sometimes a condition can exist, but you just may not be aware of it. Be sure you understand the reality of your situation.

Stories are important to any culture. They teach important lessons that we all need to learn.

Be creative!

April 21, 2010

35

Unprepared

When I graduated high school I was vastly unprepared for college: not socially, psychologically, or educationally. I had gone to a high school where we didn't have much of a library. We stocked our library with books the white school no longer wanted. We weren't required to read more than what was in our textbooks—some didn't read that. There was no library in Hallsville, Texas that I was aware of. I'm not sure if Blacks were allowed to use the public libraries in Longview or Marshall, towns nearby—I never tried to enter any of them. I wasn't aware of any bookstores in Longview or Marshall. We wrote few papers or essays, and took even fewer field trips. Our elementary, junior, and high school years were filled with times of staring out the window surrounded by too much downtime.

My mother and father never came to school to see about me, and the school could do with me whatever they wanted. My father was out of town and my mother believed in keeping herself isolated. My mother went to the eighth grade and my father went to the second grade and dropped out to help on the farm. They didn't understand how or believe that an education could benefit their children. In any regard, they weren't prepared to give them an education. My parents were working-class individuals. There was very little unity or support within the family. We lived in a rural area without indoor plumbing, gas, or telephone.

We only had a part-time counselor, and she didn't spend a great deal of time with me discussing my future. Not much was expected of me because of my background. I'm sure the teachers informed her of the students who had promise, and those who didn't. I was considered with not much promise. I was rated number three out of a class of eighty. I don't think anyone expected me to attend college because of my background. My rating was probably considered some kind of fluke. I didn't know how to apply for scholarships, and no one gave me any help.

I received no preparation for the ACT. I knew nothing of classes that would help prepare me for the test. All of a sudden one day the principal told us we needed to take the test if we wanted to go to college, and what it would cost. I paid to take the test, but had no idea what it would be about. Several weeks from that time we took a bus to Longview and took the test at Letourneau College.

I remember not having any breakfast, and getting hungry about three-fourths the way through the test. I was so hungry that I got tired of taking the test, and just began guessing an alphabet. I didn't even read the questions. Even so, I made a good enough score on the test to be admitted to the college I had planned to attend, but I often wondered how well I would have done had I took the test on a full stomach, and not simply guessed at many of the answers without reading the questions.

Somehow I always wanted to go to college. I imitated some of my friends, and I knew they were planning to attend college. Also, my cousin was teaching science at our high school. I kind of wanted to imitate him, although I didn't exactly want to teach. I chose a college after talking to an individual in the class ahead of me. He told me it was a good school and he was considering it. I decided to apply. I applied and was accepted. Even though I tried to imitate some of my friends, I didn't want to attend the same school as they did. I had heard too much negative talk about the school they were planning to attend.

Nobody in my family, or any of my relatives came to see me graduate. Also there were no gifts from any of them. I don't remember getting congratulations from any of them.

My brother had bought me a car when I was a sophomore in high school, but by this time the car was in the worst of condition. I figured I would be better off without taking the car to school with me, so I gave the car back to my brother before going to school. If I had been thinking I would have traded it in on a better one. But at the time I figured a car wouldn't be necessary. I think my brother took it as a personal affront when I gave the car back to him, because after that he discontinued all support for some reason. I was hoping he would help me through college financially. I continued to visit him, but he didn't provide any more support. He had supported me throughout my elementary, junior, and high school days.

Regardless of the situation, during this time reasonable loans were available. I managed to get a National Defense Student Loan for the four years. I was also the recipient of a monthly stipend from Social Security. During this period Social Security would give a student a monthly stipend if their father had retired and was getting Social Security. The Nixon administration discontinued this policy. Receiving Social Security benefits were most beneficial to me. It provided me with spending money, while my loan paid my tuition, room and board, and books. The Social Security stipend also bought me a few clothes, and an occasional meal at the Tiki Burger. The Tiki Burger had some delicious food.

We were integrated in the classrooms and in the dormitories; although, most Black students had Black roommates. Otherwise, it was segregated. Blacks were not encouraged to participate in fraternities, clubs, and organizations. When we attended sporting events we usually seated ourselves in different sections, even though the teams were fully integrated. I could tell some stories about particular incidents of racism, but don't have the space or time here.

I did fairly well in my class work, but spent most of my time studying. I was so far behind that I needed to spend my time in the books. I hated to go home because my parents still didn't have telephone or indoor plumbing. I stayed on campus when I could. Sometimes the dorms would close for the holidays, and I had to go home and face the music.

One brother came to visit me once during the four years I was at the school. I think the only reason he came was because his in-laws lived in that town. One sister sent me twenty-five dollars during these four years. None of the others came to visit, wrote me a letter, or sent a care package. They were totally oblivious to where I was or what I was doing. As well, none of them came to see me graduate.

When I graduated I was no more prepared for the world than I was when I entered college. I had no idea what I would do with my life. I had no money and had no choice but to join the military. I couldn't afford to get an apartment, and didn't want to go back to Hallsville and live in the country with my parents. None of my other relatives offered me a place to live until I could get on my feet. I had spent every dime I had on getting through college. I wanted to go on to graduate school, but only applied to the University of Texas, and was unsuccessful at getting accepted. I had big plans for myself.

It's hard to say my subsequent difficulties were based on any one factor. Sometimes I want to say, if I only had a little better socialization in college my life would have been better. But I was isolated as a child, stuttered, received inadequate early education, lack of family support, and spent too much time in my dorm room without adequate socialization in college. All of these things contributed to my problems.

All the while I kept thinking, one day I would have a son, and what I would want to do for him. I hope Frances and I have given you a background such that life won't ever catch you unprepared.

Whatever move you make, be sure you are prepared for the next step. Work hard and hang in there!

Stay goal oriented!

April 28, 2010

36

Do Your Best: Starting a New Educational Tradition

I know you remember the Cub Scott's motto, *do your best*. All anyone can expect is that you'll, *do your best*. I always felt that you have lots of ability, and by your high school record you have proven that you have the ability to do well. I only ask that you live up to your potential.

They say a person is likely to pass on to their offspring what they have been able to accomplish. Things somehow get passed on from one generation to another. If your parents lived a comfortable life style, you will be able to live a more comfortable life style.

I don't know much about my grandparents, I only met my paternal grandmother. She was almost ninety years old when I met her. She didn't have much energy, and was kind of cold and distant. If she wanted to speak to me she would talk through my father. She didn't have much education, I'm sure of that fact. In fact, neither of my grandparents had much education. All of them had been sharecroppers for most of their lives. Even my mother and father spent the earlier part of their marriage as sharecroppers.

My mother was raised on a farm in a small town in East Texas. She didn't get any further than the eighth grade. There was no high school in the immediate farm area, and there was no way for her to travel to the city to attend high school. She then went to work on her parents' farm. She stayed around that farm until she got married at the age of twenty-one. Part of her duties was to plow in the fields, by using a team of mules. I don't know much about her life on the farm. All I know is what she told me, and what I can interpolate. We had many discussions while sitting by a warm fire on those cold winter nights in East Texas. My grandfather had managed to acquire his own land, and didn't have to sharecrop any more. There were at least seven children in my grandfather's first marriage. My mother was the forth child. He later married again after my mother's mother died, and had four other children by his new wife. My mother barely finished elementary school, and had no opportunity for going to college. My mother spent the rest of her life raising ten children, and tending a small-dirt farm. She lived her life in isolation with nothing but a pig trail to her house. She gave no further thoughts to getting a better education.

My father was the eighth child in a family of sixteen children. He was raised in sharecropping situations, as his father never managed to acquire any land. They spent their time going from one sharecropping situation to another. My father only finished the second grade. He then quit school and went to work doing chores on the farm. He eventually left the farm and went to work in an oil refinery on the Gulf Coast.

Neither of my parents encouraged any of their children to seek higher education. They were content with having them help out on the farm until they could leave. My sisters and brothers never received training for anything but managing that small farm. Most of them never accomplished anything but raising their families, and going from one menial job to another.

I saw and heard a lot as I grew up. But at least I was motivated from what I saw to strive for an education. No one encouraged me, not even my sisters, brothers, or parents. Somehow I badly wanted to get an education. I could see how not having an education affected the lives of my sisters and brothers.

It was hard for me, but I made it through elementary, high school, and college. I remember some days in elementary school when I had no money for lunch. In college I had some hard days, but I never seriously wanted to give up.

That's why I want to see you do well. There was a lot of hidden potential in my family. I want to see you be all that you can be. Don't ever try to take short cuts. Strive to make every effort to fully utilize your potential.

I know I didn't do much with the latter part of my life, but at least I received a stipend from the government, and was able to help take care of my family—that is a start. However, I do regret not accomplishing more with my level of education. Without getting an education I wouldn't have been able to accomplish what I did. There's no way around it, getting an education is better in the end. *They say it's better to have an education, and not need one, than to need and education and not have one.* I believe this old saying is true.

I would like to see you be the seed for a new generation, but don't take this too seriously, I don't want you carrying unnecessary weight on your shoulder. Start a strong tradition of education in the family from this point forward.

Be aware!!!!!!!!!!!!!

May 5, 2010

37

Cry a Few Tears for Me

When my father died my mother called and said, "Johnnie's gone." She called him by his given name; he had no nickname that we called him. Some of my brothers did appropriately call him John. Nicknames weren't very common in our family. I remember shedding a few tear, but my father was never much of a father in my life.

When I was a few years old he took a job on the Gulf Coast, in a town called Texas City. It was right after World War II, and jobs in the plants on the coast were plentiful.

I heard my mother and father talking once. They said my father got into an argument with a white man over her, pulled a gun on him, and the man told him he was going to kill him if he didn't leave town. My father caught the first bus for the coast, and took the first job he could get. He was at that job until he retired.

Another reason my father left was because jobs were difficult to get in that small town. He felt he could better take care of his family by working on the coast. Lots of men did it. It was also difficult for my father to get to a job. There was no transportation. There was nothing but a three-mile trail to our house, and no way to get to the city once he negotiated the dew, tree limbs, ditches, and streams. This trail led to a two-lane, winding, hill-ridden, curvaceous highway. There were two cities: one twenty miles to the south (45,000), and another twenty miles to the north (2,000).

As I grew up I visited him on the coast. I didn't like Texas City. At times the air was so thick with sulfur and other chemicals that you could cut it with a knife. Even in Texas City my father didn't spend much time with me. He pawned me off to the sons of one of his girlfriends. They could have been my brothers. He never admitted this was the case, but I could read between the lines. I always had my suspicions. Some folks said he had several women on the coast, and at least several children. It was clear that he had a close relationship with one family. Once he brought several children home with him. He had a hard time explaining that to my mother, and she was very angry. She finally realized what was going on. I still don't know what possessed him to bring them home.

I had a lot of duties on the farm, and couldn't spend much time away from the farm, but I did spend a few weeks during several summers on the coast.

He never took me places as I grew up. We never caught a baseball or football, or even went to a football game. He never even visited the school I attended. We barely even talked. When he came home all we ever talked about was doing the chores. Mostly we just didn't say much. It was like everything was understood.

He never talked to me about getting an education or how it could benefit me. He didn't even encourage me in school. He should have been aware that I couldn't stay on the farm forever.

My father made every effort to get my mother to move to Texas City, but she continued to resist. She felt she had her little shotgun shack, food to eat, a place to lay her head, and she wasn't leaving it. I'm not sure why my father didn't simply give up on her and move completely to Texas City, but he must have felt some sort of obligation or attachment.

Later when my father retired, he came back home. We still never talked very much. When we visited anyone I always stayed in the car while he went inside to visit. He spent the rest of his life going back and forth between East Texas and the coast. He couldn't quite give up Texas City.

I never really knew him, so I had little feeling for a real person when he died. I had a few tears for him, but I never felt that close to him.

I know my relationship with my father has affected my relationship with you, and I know I haven't always been there for you. They say relationships tend to get carried over from one generation to another.

When I die I hope you will shed a few tears for me, because that will mean to me that I had been a meaningful, living, breathing thing in your life.

I hope that you will be able to have a better relationship with your son. By maintaining a better relationship with your son you can bring these pathological father-to-son relationships in our family to an end. They have existed for years in our family. Older generations weren't that concerned about it. As long as they had food, clothing, and shelter they were happy.

Be concerned!!!!!!!!!!!!!!

May 12, 2010

38

His-Story

Keep the thoughts in these emails to yourself. There're some people who're not ready for what I have to say. I want you to know the truth. If you speak up in class about certain issues in certain ways, you might make some unnecessary enemies. Professors aren't going to give you certain information; you'll have to read for yourself at a later date. That's why you get an education, so you can figure out what you need to read on your own. College is only a beginning. European Americans present information from their point of view. It's what Black activist refer to as "his-story," as opposed to "our-story."

They don't like you to give a different perspective than the one they've been trained to teach you. Remember you're attending a European American school rather than a historically Black school. Be careful what you say, if you have a feeling it will go against the grain, stay out of trouble, and keep in good standing. Don't give any of your professors a hard time, but keep what I say in the back of your mind.

Always answer the questions on your tests according to what the professor says, and according to what is reflected by your assigned readings. I know what I say might be different from what you have learned in school; since most of your teachers were/are white, and the Black ones tend to stay away from controversial issue.

My teachers were all Black in elementary, junior high, and high school. I can never remember any of them discussing a controversial issue. They were probably afraid of losing their jobs. Teachers who spoke out on controversial issues were frequently blackballed, and they would have difficulty finding another job. They knew what and what not to say. I'm sure they were schooled in this regard. My history teacher avoided the subject of Black history like it was the plague. We rarely had even a Black speaker for Black history week; more than likely we had a European American speaker. So they taught us only what they were told to teach, which was as little as possible. They mainly just sat with us until we were able to graduate. We didn't get much conventional wisdom, nor did we get much of a Black perspective.

I was in school during the Civil Rights Movement, but I can't remember one of my teachers saying anything about the movement. They all kept quiet as a mouse. Even when the movement threatened to flare up in a town nearby, none of my teachers spoke up about it. My history and government teacher was even quieter than the rest.

Many students did get frustrated and dropped out. I was frustrated in school but never considered dropping out. I had a sense that I wasn't getting all that I was supposed to, but had nothing to compare my education to. It was only a vague sense that something was missing in my educational process. I knew I wanted to go on to college, and that I would need some kind of a high school degree. I therefore toughed it out, and gave no consideration to doing otherwise. I had no other options.

In college it was rare that a book written by a Black man was used for a class. And they definitely would never use a controversial book written by a Black man. They finally got one Black professor during my senior year. I got college from a European American's perspective, which wasn't that bad, but you need the other perspective. If you're going to go to a European American school rather than an African American one, it would be good if you could read some Black books in your spare time, and also attend some Black lectures. Many of the European American professors are aware of the African American's perspective in regard to history, but are reluctant to teach it. They also stay away from controversy.

For young Blacks to see the world from a totally European American's perspective is bound to be confusing. They see nothing of themselves in the images they encounter. It's bound to take a toll on their self-esteem, self-worth, and self-image. It's good for them at some point to get something of their own culture from this education. But don't be confused, you need this European American education—especially when it's the only game in town.

You need to somehow stay in touch with African American culture. I waited until after I graduated from college to begin reading about this perspective. This was a bit late, but not too late. I started by attending lectures in the city, and also reading books about African Americans whenever I could.

At this point you of course need to focus on reading your assignments. I'm sure you have your work cut out for you just doing that. Whatever you do don't neglect your studies. You need that degree, and will need good grades if you want to go any further. They want you to have at least a "B" average if you want to get into a good graduate school. Some graduate schools want at least a 3.5 on a four-point system. The competition for graduate schools is becoming increasingly competitive. That's why you don't need to make any enemies by bringing up controversial ideas. If you go on to graduate school you will need references from several of your college professors.

Even if you had gone to a historically African American college or university, you still might only get mainstream thought. These schools are partially supported by other groups in many cases, and are careful what they provide is conventional wisdom. The idea is not to bite the hand that feeds you.

African Americans have to walk a tightrope in regard to their education. It's difficult for them to do a balancing act on this tightrope. On the one hand they want to get a good education, but when they seek such an education, find mostly mainstream ideas. This leaves them knowing little about their own culture. It's up to you to devise a scheme to keep yourself together, get your degree, and plan for your future.

Be intelligent about it!

May 19, 2010

39

Utilizing Your Potential

Some say a person won't be happy until they're doing what the Creator created them to do. This is why so many people are unhappy. Most of them never find out what they were created for. Everybody has something specifically they were designed to do. In other words everybody has a specific assignment on this earth, and they have the potential to be good at it. Sometimes it takes training to be good at your assignment, but everybody at least has some trainable potential in a certain area.

Remember in the Bible where each man was given so many talents. One man used his talents to increase his lot, while one other thought he would be unsuccessful and buried his talents. The moral of the story is that you must use the talents you're given to better your situation.

Some people are good at sports, some can sing well, some have mechanical or technological abilities, some can sew well, some are extremely verbal, and some are generally good at academics. Sometimes people have several areas in which they could possibly be good at with some training. I believe that you are generally good at academics. I don't know what specific area of academics you're best at; that is for you to find out while you're in college. I'm sure high school gave you some ideas, but you can further refine that knowledge. I do believe that you have good general intelligence.

No matter what you major in you can use it to do what you're good at. The purpose of getting an education should be to help you find out what you're good at, and to help you learn how to think. That's why the curriculum in college is so broad, so you can explore and figure out what you're good at. High school should have helped you to have some idea about your abilities, and college should help you refine those ideas. Even lower-level education is supposed to help you figure out what you're good at. Some people major in a certain area in college, and become a millionaire in a totally different area.

Some people can be trained to do just about anything, while others find it virtually impossible to learn certain skills. That's where general intelligence comes into play. I don't believe in wasting my time trying to develop a skill in an area where I have no talent.

In school I tried everything. I had no idea of what I was good at. I discovered late in life that I possibly could have had some potential in writing. Not only do I feel I could have some talent in this area, but find that I like doing it. In high school I never learned much about the finer points of English, and had no idea that I had any talent in this area. Nobody ever took the time to teach me any English, and I wasn't aware enough to pursue it on my own. I embarrassed myself many times by trying to do things in which I had absolutely no talent. This is because my high school wasn't set up to help you find what you were good at. It's good to not only have talent in an area, but to like doing it, if you're going to pursue it as a career. Some people are good at certain things but have no appreciation for them.

Find out what you're good at and what you like doing. Then you'll know what you want to pursue as a career. Some people say find something that you would do for free if you had to, and if you're good at it pursue it as a career. This is what you need to do. But take your time; you have plenty of time to figure out what you want to do with your life.

Find something you like, in an area that you have talent, and that pays well. Since everybody likes money, you must consider that aspect as well. It takes money to make a living.

Whatever you do, use your potential to the best of your ability.

Be sure you know in what area your potential lies!!!!!!!

May 26, 2010

40

On God and Religion

I have never talked to you before about religion. I figured your mother had a close reign on that area. One reason I haven't, in addition to my general communication problem, is because I didn't want to contradict your mother's teachings, and what you were learning in the church. Some religious training is better than none at all, and it's rare that anyone says going to church affected them in a negative manner. I believe there is a lot of value in having a strong religious background. We can see this by the fact that people who go to church have a higher rate of graduation from high school, and generally stay out of trouble or prison. There's something to be said for the strong values being taught in the church.

I believe in a type of god, not the kind that most church people praise and worship. It's my belief that man created the concept of God over a long period of time. He created the concept of God because he needed something to believe in that was greater than himself. Out of his dreams, wishes, fantasies, thoughts, and existential longings he came up with this idea. Out of this need he came up with this omnipotent, omnipresent, all-seeing, and all-knowing deity.

The principle function of the religion our oppressor gave to us is to separate us from the reality of our own spirituality. We have taken the truth for a lie, and the lie for the truth—with respect to religion.

Rather than a god, I believe there is a Balance in the Universe. If you want to equate this with a god be my guest.

There was an explosion in the universe in ancient times. Out of this explosion came a natural balance. Everything in the universe is in balance. Matter, the stars, planets, rivers, lakes, and oceans are in balance. Even our bodies are in a system of balance. Animals are arranged in a system of balance. Inorganic material in the universe is in a system of balance. For every action there is an equal and opposite reaction. What goes around comes around. These sayings denote this Balance in the Universe.

When we go contrary to this Balance we have to pay a price. For example, when we smoke heavily over a period of time we get lung cancer; if we go in deep water, and can't swim, we will usually drown; if we stay outside in the cold for long periods in our bare feet, we will either catch a cold or pneumonia. When we transgress against this Balance we are likely to pay a price. There is no devil harassing us, or a higher power waiting to punish us. The only power is this system of checks and balances.

All the talk about tithing and giving a tenth of your earnings to God is just something set up by man to benefit the church. This information may be found in the Bible, but the Bible was written by men and translated many times. I wouldn't be surprised what was found in the Bible. It is a compilation of fables, allegories, and folktales. Much of it is nevertheless good to live by. The reason the preacher emphasize tithing so much is because the church system depends on tithing. Without tithing the church couldn't survive. Ministers only tell you what will benefit them and the church. Everything they say is designed to keep you putting your money in the collection plate. The preachers sometime have some good information, but we don't have to settle for their religious mythology.

The idea of a god as put forth by Westerners has done more damage to Blacks than any other concept in the history of man. Believing in a blonde, blue-eyed god is a detriment to Black people. And most people still believe that God was either a European or a Jew. If you truly believe that your god is in the image of a people who have done everything possible to destroy you, and you must appeal to this god for most of what you need on a daily basis, you are bound to feel inferior and that whites are superior.

But we have been taught to believe in this blonde, blue-eyed god. We say in some cases that God has no color, but when we close our eyes, I believe we still see this blonde, blue-eyed god. It's almost impossible to do otherwise after such severe conditioning. I can remember a picture of this blonde, blue-eyed Jesus hanging on our family room wall, and similar pictures hanging in various churches.

Most people on earth have a concept of their god that represents their own image. It is only Blacks that have such a concept of their god. The Europeans had to have such a concept of their god in order to maintain their superiority, and our inferiority. It's what any right thinking people would do. Why would a people let their representation of God be in the image of another people who had tried to destroy them on every level of their existence?

God is not Black or white, but is a force in the universe. It's backward to walk around believing that God is a blonde-headed, blue-eyed European. Such misinformation will never lead you to true knowledge of yourself, and you will probably always have an inferiority complex if you believe this. No matter what preachers say we must stay in touch with reality. Though, most of them say, it doesn't matter what color God is.

It's important to know history. Take a course in World History, and take some Black History courses. European religion was passed on to Blacks from the slave master. Although, Africans had their own concept of religion before other groups came to their shores. We have been passing on a European concept of religion ever since. Most of us have never taken the time to question it because most of us do need something to believe in that is bigger than ourselves. If you need something to believe in—believe in yourself.

Remember, knowledge is cumulative, and is obtained by getting a little at a time, and eventually putting it all together. You will be surprised what you can obtain, in the way of knowledge, by reading a little at a time. It is the only way to get it.

In addition, most of us don't realize that even this religion that was refurbished and given to us in slavery was copied from Egyptian myth. When Europeans came to Africa over 10,000 years ago they found a spirituality that was worthy of imitation. They copied this spirituality and mixed it with their own concepts to come up with the Holy Bible.

Religion is good for some people, because they like the idea that somebody who never really existed died on a cross to save their souls. They like this idea because they don't like to take responsibility for themselves. They don't like to carry their own burden. Letting someone else carry their burden makes life more convenient for them.

Your mother wouldn't like my sharing this information with you, but it's time that you were exposed to various ideas that exist in the world. Your mother firmly believes in the Bible. I'm not pressuring you to think like I do, just to expose you to the ideas. I know it's not your responsibility to carry my vision; I want you to have a vision of your own.

Be careful what you say in class, no matter what I say; these emails are just for your information. You can make a lot of enemies by saying things that other people are not ready for. I encourage you to read as much as possible, but don't read extra materials when it will be to the detriment of you studies. Your class work comes first, in all cases.

Be critical!!!!!!!!!!!!!!

June 2, 2010

41

Black Men Set Up to Fail

This set up began over 10,000 years ago when other groups first appeared on the shores of Africa. These groups presented themselves as superior and Africans as inferior. We permitted them to become involved in our political, marital, economic, social, and educational institutions. Soon they began to dismantle these institutions. After a while we loss touch with our own norms and values; we began to lack norms and became confused.

This process of dismantling our culture was so successful that we were vulnerable to the slave trade. We had become so confused, chaotic, and disorganized.

On the ships and on the trek to the ships we lost our sense of potency and manhood. We were badly mistreated as less than human, and were degraded in the worse way.

In slavery we were sent from plantation to plantation, used as studs and not allowed to take responsibility for our own families. We were treated as property and used for breeding purposes. We weren't allowed to marry or to have any say about our offspring. Not allowed to accumulate property. We could be sold and separated from our families at any time. This caused us to be quick today to leave our families and to be slow at forming family attachments.

After slavery things remained much the same. We were free but had no property or accumulated wealth to sustain ourselves. We became sharecroppers, and were in the same economic situation as in slavery. We were behind the eight ball and had no way to catch up. In addition there were still much prejudice, racism, and bigotry. We lived substandard lives as second-class citizens. There were never equal opportunities or a level-playing field.

At this point we've been without equal opportunities for education. We lack employment opportunities, still discriminated against at every opportunity, and discriminated against in the criminal justice system. The first hired and the last fired. We continue to be disadvantaged when it comes to getting appropriate educational equipment and supplies. We are 13% of the population, but are 60% of the prison population.

Today, prisons are making a business out of young Black men being incarcerated. Corporations are taking over the prison systems. It seems that society is delighted to see young Black men going to prison in order to support the Prison-Industrial Complex. At this point we have too many young Black men in prison. Black men have been set up to take this hit.

Since they can't get regular jobs at a desirable level, they have no choice but prison. I believe a lot of young men see a place to sleep and three meals a day as desirable to living in the conditions of society. The educational system undereducates them, and the system for Blacks is vastly underfunded. There is little for them to do except get trapped by the prison system. The only jobs available for those with their skills are those in drugs and other illegal activities, which quickly leads them into the prison system. Once in the prison system they learn how to commit bigger and better crimes. Professional sports and entertainment will only provide a few jobs. The rest will have to survive the best way they can. Most Black men are not attracted to low-paying jobs in the fast-food industry. The only jobs they qualify for are the labor intensive and the unskilled.

Once they get out of prison it's even more difficult to get a job. The only thing to do is to get involved in crime and end up going back to prison. This whole process then becomes a revolving door.

I say young Black men going to prison are a set up from the beginning. They're set up to fail in this society in so many ways. Don't be a victim of this society's intent to cripple Black males. You need an education to overcome this detrimental process, and you have made a good start. Keep up the good work!

You not only need a good education, but to keep your head straight. You also need to know who you are, whose you are, where you're going, and where you came from.

Be adaptive!!!!!!!!!!!!!

June 9, 2010

42

Modern-Day Racism and Blackism

We'd expect that racism in this country has decreased in some cases. After all, don't we have an African-American president? But racism is and will continue to be with us. It's felt that under certain conditions people feel comfortable excluding certain people from their inner circle and including others. If people aren't excluded on the basis of race or skin color; it'll be size of nose, color of hair, size of feet, or color of eyes, etc. Here are just a few of the many ways in which racism is still a factor in the Black community.

1). Banks are reluctant to give Black people loans to go into business, or to buy property. When they do it seems they are unwilling to give them as much as they give other groups. They still want to give Blacks pennies while giving other groups millions. It's as if they feel Blacks are still children and can only manage a small amount of money.

Eddy Murphy, a famous comedian, did a skit on "Saturday Night Live" a few years ago, where when others came into a bank for a loan, the loan officer took out a suitcase filled with money and handed it to them without question. When a Black man came in he wanted to know what kind of collateral he had. Whereas this is an over exaggeration, it's not too far fetched.

2). There's a difference in the sentencing of Blacks and other groups in the so-called criminal justice system. Other groups get less time than Blacks for committing a similar offense. When a Black kills a member of another group he can look forward to a lot of time. When a member of another group kills a Black not much time is involved. Even when a Black kills a Black not much time is involved. It's been this way since Blacks came to this country.

Blacks who get caught with crack cocaine will do a longer sentence than other groups who get caught with powdered cocaine—the substance from which crack is derived. At one time five grams of crack cocaine would get you the same sentence as five-hundred grams of powdered cocaine. Blacks are more likely to use crack cocaine.

Other groups usually commit more white-collar crime, and will get less of a sentence than Blacks who usually commit crimes against persons or property.

3). Less money is still invested in inner-city schools. They're still investing less in infrastructure, books, materials, and supplies; much as was done shortly after the Civil War. They use the excuse that Blacks in inner-city schools have a lower-tax base. It's time to invest equally in all schools.

4). When Blacks try to enter the system at any point, the big word they use is "qualified." They try to tell you that you aren't qualified in some way. It's a catch word. You're not qualified for college, for a loan, for a job, etc. If Blacks can't get an equal education, or a decent job, naturally they're not going to be qualified in most other ways.

5). I still believe it's easier for other groups to become officers in the United States military. Blacks have to be exceptional, while other groups only average to become an officer.

Blackism is when Blacks discriminate against each other. This situation is still an ever-present factor in our lives. Blacks have been conditioned to self-hate, so that when we're frustrated we turn our destructiveness upon one another.

1). Blacks in many cases don't support one another. We often have little loyalty, love, lack unity, and fail to consolidate resources.

2). Blacks hesitate to do business with each other. We too often feel that other groups' ice is colder than Black ice. We feel there's something wrong with the products a Black man is selling, while buying the same products from other groups. If all else is in order, we say we don't like the attitude of the Black merchant.

3). Blacks hire other groups to provide services to their community rather than hire Black men. We do so when young Black men are standing on the corner and playing video games. How can we expect to build our communities when we're doing things like this? Anyone doing such a thing can't see the larger picture. We need to train and provide opportunities for young Black men in carpentry, masonry, electrical works, bricklaying, air conditioning, heating, and plumbing, etc. The basic services needed for a community to survive should be supported and engaged in by young Black men. A community must be self-sustaining.

4). Many Blacks still consider personality rather than the ability to get a job done. Other groups will forget about personality if one can get a job done. With some Blacks they consider personality first: if they don't like your personality you won't get much further.

Thoroughly consider all of your behavior. Don't hate—celebrate.

Be comfortable with everyone!!!!!!!

June 16, 2010

43

One Final Note

I know I've been called retarded and everything else under the sun. But I guess under certain conditions a person would have a tendency to call another retarded. I can't say some of this name calling wasn't justified; I realize the reasons for some of the name calling. I want you to know the facts of the situation.

I had absolutely no preschool educational training. My mother, father, sisters, nor brothers attempted to provide any such training. There was no such thing as kindergarten, head start, or day care in my community; if there had been it would have been unlikely I would have been sent. I also stuttered severely. I was isolated at the end of a three-mile trail that led to a blacktopped, two-lane highway, in which there were twenty miles both north and south to small towns. We didn't get a graded dirt road until I was in first grade.

I didn't start to school until I was almost seven-years old. If your birthday came after September, you had to wait until the next year to enter school. Mine came in October.

Once I started school, I remember teachers didn't pay me much attention, I simply floated along. I do remember that none of my teachers ever tried to show me how to form my letters, and I got no such help at home. This is a fact which is still evident in my cursive writing today.

In the fifth grade my teacher doubled as the music teacher for the entire school. A great deal of the time we spent listening to her music students practice for upcoming concerts. This left her fifth-grade class neglected. But she was generally a good teacher. When we were in class we usually got down to business.

I was doing pretty good until I got to the sixth grade, and was placed in a teacher's class who doubled as teacher and band director. I joined the marching band because he needed another warm body. I spent a lot of time traveling with the marching band and out of class. In the evening instead of staying in class with the other students, I was sent to the band room with my main teacher.

In the seventh grade they bumped this teacher from sixth to seventh grade, and I was unfortunate enough to get him for my seventh-grade teacher. This year the band director would go to the band room for the morning hour next to noon. He would take me with him. I missed a whole year of Texas History because I went to the band room with him. The principal allowed me to do this. He was the one teaching the class on Texas History. After all this, the band director failed to attempt to teach me to read one note of music. Once in the seventh grade the teacher gave us an assignment, and I was so disillusioned with the system that I picked a piece of paper off the floor and turned it in. The teacher accepted it and put a check in his record book, and on the paper itself. This was the only assignment I remember getting in the sixth and seventh grades.

In the eighth grade my class had approximately eighty students. It was divided into two sections. It seems to me that the teacher put all her efforts into the class that they considered had more promise. The class that I was in was considered to have less promise. She had the other class first, and when she got to us I believe she didn't want to repeat herself. I would sometimes hear one particular guy talking about the interesting things they did in class. When she got to us we did absolutely nothing.

In the tenth grade I recall an algebra I class being divided so that I was in a class of all boys who was considered to have less promise. I am not certain of this but I felt the teacher dummied down the materials to fit that particular group, and skipped over the more complicated materials. The teacher was excellent in spite of this situation.

I regret that there was no attempt to teach us grammar either in elementary or high school. We wrote few papers, barely read any novels, and didn't even practice writing. We weren't encouraged to read. There wasn't much of a library at the school, and the little town didn't have a library that I knew about. The towns nearby had libraries but I don't know if Blacks were allowed to enter. Most of my time, except for math and science, was spent as downtime. I sat and stared out the window for numerous hours. We all acted as if that was perfectly normal.

There came a time in the eleventh grade when the classes got reshuffled, and I took most of my classes with the students who were considered to have more promise. This included such classes as chemistry, geometry, physics, and algebra II. These classes were top of the line as far as our school went. We didn't have pre-calculus, calculus, trigonometry, algebra and trigonometry, or a second class in chemistry or physics. But it was too-little-too-late, and the damage had already been done by the goings on in earlier years.

I guess after all the damage that had been done by not getting any preschool education, starting to school late, not being paid much attention in general, not being able go get speech therapy, then encountering the dark ages in the sixth and seventh grades, and neglect from then on; I can see why I might have been considered a little retarded, no matter if I did still perform better than most of the other students. My severe stuttering didn't help to improve my image. My folks couldn't afford speech therapy, nor did we have transportation to where one might be, even if there was one who practiced in the surrounding area. There were no speech pathologists or speech courses at the school.

I hope your mother and I, and the educational system, have prepared you better than I was prepared. I realize that I grew up in a different circumstance, place, and time; and that things have changed a great deal in most places. I know your mother and I tried our best. You attended a good high school and are attending a good college. I hope you will make the best of your opportunities.

Be positive!!!!!!!!!

June 23, 2010

44

A New Vision for an Old Man

I started writing you these emails on August 26, 2009, when you enrolled in school. I wasn't too pleased with the school, but realized it was a compromise. I have been sending you these emails because I wanted you to know that you're somebody. In your mother's sight, in my sight, in your brother's sight, in your relatives' sight, and in significant others' sight you are definitely somebody.

I started writing the emails because I felt there were some things we should have discussed while you were growing up that we never discussed, and hoped that we could use this opportunity to catch up on some issues. Because of my background there were some things that made it hard for me to communicate with you. I believe this to be a factor in the lives of many young Black men and their fathers. The problem comes out of our history of slavery in this country, when Black fathers weren't allowed the responsibility of being fathers. In addition, I had some personal deficiencies of my own.

They say Black children today don't know enough of the country's history, as well as Black history, or their own personal family history for that matter. I wanted to try and provide you with some of these. I wanted you to know where I came from in hopes that it would motivate you to work harder.

You should strive hard to overcome my history, and to make a better life for yourself. Every father wants his children to have a better life than he had. I tell you all these things so you can prepare yourself for a brighter future. We must constantly be aware of that proverbial ape, and how it must be content with trial and error.

I have written these emails because I don't want you to experience the same things I experienced, and if you do you will know how to respond. I hope you internalize what I have said. They say children are likely to be like their parents unless they make a conscious effort to change, and even then are likely to be like them in some ways. It's hard not to be like one's parents because of the way we're socialized in this country. I want you to make that effort and do something with your life.

I want you and Marcus to be the basis for a new generation. You have to make it better for future generations. I don't want any more generations to go through what I went through. I realize this is a heavy burden to place on any two individuals.

I want your children to live in a decent environment, to grow up in an exceptional and strong family, to get the kind of education they want, to not experience excessive emotional turmoil, to get the jobs they want, to have most of the material things they want, and to not have stress on every hand.

Unfortunately, we won't be able to protect them from discrimination and racism, because it has always been with us and I fear it will be with us for a long time to come, but maybe we can prepare them to live with it, and to build a better life in spite of it.

People can tell how you walk, talk, and act, as to whether you are serious about your future. Be sure to always make a good presentation. I wanted you to understand your history, to be motivated, and get you off to a good start in college. Treat life as if you have a mission and a purpose. Erase all your doubts and fears and get on with your life.

If you have any concerns that you want to discuss, feel free to get in contact with me or your mother. We both are always open and happy to discuss things with you. I hope I have created the kind of atmosphere where we can have open communication and dialogue from this day forward.

Lastly, I want to say, as a boy walking through the hills and valleys of my parents' fifty acre farm in East Texas, I was oblivious to the environment. At the earliest age I wasn't mindful of snakes, wolves, coyote, bobcats or wildcats. I was like Tarzan in the jungle.

Then I recall while in the Navy walking through the dense urban jungle of Boston on my way to the train station as if there were no dangers. I still hadn't learned. Luckily, I was able to survive these situations. They say *God takes care of fools and babies.*

I've been in many situations that as a young man I had no business in. Be mindful of your environment. Don't hang around places that can be deleterious to your health. By hanging around such places they can hasten your existence on this planet.

With that I will end my emails. It's time for you to fly on your own. That is not to say that you haven't always done this. I'll continue to be in contact with you, but won't continue to write you an email once a week. I hope you have benefited by these emails.

Take care.

We live in an awesome world. Make it an awesome college life. Peace to you; may God bless you. Live simply. Love generously. Care deeply. Speak kindly.

Be aggressive and strong, yet sensitive and understanding!!!!!!!!!

Never, ever, give up!

Made in the USA
Monee, IL
04 November 2026

67380488R00098